THE WISE LISTEN

THE WISE LISTEN

Copyright © Pino Deufemia 2010

All Rights Reserved
No part of this book may be reproduced in any form by photocopying or by any electronic or mechanical means, including information storage and retrieval systems, without permission in writing from the copyright owner and publisher of this book.

ISBN 978-0-9567350-0-3

Cover photography by Pino Deufemia

Printing and distribution by www.lulu.com

Humanities profoundest questions that all the prophets and wise men before me could not answer are answered HERE. Before we begin I would like to add some words of wisdom from one of such wise men.

Do not believe in anything simply because you have heard it. Do not believe in anything simply because it is spoken and rumoured by many. Do not believe in anything simply because it is found written in your religious books. Do not believe in anything merely on the authority of your teachers and elders. Do not believe in traditions because they have been handed down through many generations, but after observation and analysis, when you find anything that agrees with reason and is likely to lead to the good and benefit of one and all, then accept it and look up to it. (Buddha)
- BEHOLD -

THE WISE LISTEN

What you are about to read is the **only** concept in the world of its kind, in the history of mankind, neither before or ever to be in the near future, until mankind develops its understanding in acknowledging an existence of what is hereby written. I have stumbled across some scriptures in a similar vein which cannot be understood by the many; therefore I have simplified what I write so all can now understand.

I would like to make clear that this book is not simply based on society's creation of religion, it has been written with the intention for mankind to understand the balance of the world and how to regulate and work with it in harmony. It is also explained in both earthly and spiritual realms. The words, God, Devil, Heaven and Hell have been chosen to simplify and symbolise the existence of negative and positive elements and energies and for being most commonly recognised.

I previously had hardly any educated knowledge of what I write, as this has come to me by the means of channelling a Holy Spirit/Benevolent life force and through secrets stumbled across whilst researching if there was a truth behind what I had channelled, these truths are found all around us if one opens their mind and looks.

I believe that I have been specifically chosen among many, this weighs heavy on one man alone.

In the quest to write this book I suffer the inherited abandonment of mankind, my closest will scorn me and question my sanity, not questioning the possibility it may be they who lack understanding and refuse the will to reason.

When one stumbles across the cure to life's destructive elements reaching a sense of exhilaration in its discovery, and eagerly wanting to share and pass the wisdom onto those I love most, it is difficult beyond explanation to then have to standby and watch them repel my hand, my intentions were to reach out and stop them falling, resulting in feelings of frustration and anger towards myself in not finding a solution. The burning inside me cannot be quenched, and I know I will carry the truth to my death, ironically only my death being the awakening for many, as the psychology of mankind would only then dismiss the person, allowing the mystery of the writing left behind as a QUEST, ironically, then being subjected to a multitude of interpretations due to my absence.

Yet I am grateful, as it has given me a guiding light, releasing me from all the worlds' darkest moments. I believe it is my quest to pass on and allow humanity the knowledge that only a few worldly selected individuals know. This can be the beginning of your enlightenment; this can be the beginning of your life.

Those of you who will attempt to open their minds and listen rather than judge what is written, to understand or have a desire for knowledge, will be enlightened. I would recommend you all take this opportunity to read this book, as I am sure it will trigger a thought with the hope of changing your life for the better.

After reading this book and following its contents as a guide, those of you '**will**' reawaken a divinity of lost mystical powers.

*"The most beautiful thing we can experience is the mysterious.
It is the source of all true art and science"*
(Albert Einstein)

Be the change you want to see in the world.
(Mahatma Gandhi)

No one can say that what they know is an infallible fact but that it is a current truth.

Introduction – Paragraphs from this book entwine and show the gradual process of knowledge leading to the final printed understanding, making it preferable to read from beginning to end, to read it otherwise may allow paragraphs to be misinterpreted and misunderstood.

This is a verse I wrote on the subject of birth

The planet is a mental asylum and I arrived here like a shit down the pan from some psychopathic shistos with no will to prevent the splash drop. Like a person sentenced to death for a crime he did not commit, but once judged by a race of unseeing fools with the intelligence of a trained monkey to which they are also the sentenced. Although they have eyes they are blind and lobotomised by the society in witch they live. If you were an ant, do you know of the human races existence, as we are like the ant but must believe different because we are the intelligent....said the ant !!!

BIRTH

Non-religious Birth

A child is born, not any child but you! A child can be born anywhere these days so I will not give you a full list, and allow you to use your imagination, just some examples include: - hospitals, homes, cars, in a pool of water, ambulance, some just squat somewhere…. 'A barn'!

You do not have the choice of wanting to be born or not, your parents choose this, just like you might one day and you can be sure that they had a great time making you!

So there you are, having won one of your greatest achievements "the sperm race", so if there is nothing else that you win in your life, you can always look back on that.

Religious Birth

We come back to the question, did you or did you not, have the choice of being born? Where were you prior to your birth? Were you in heaven? Were you in hell or were you an entity in some unseen dimension? Did you exist at all? Well, if you did have a choice, you certainly cannot remember having one, and not only being born, but the choice to whom you were born. Well, I know that if I did have a choice of family, I made an intelligent decision there! I could not have chosen a more loving family. Or, was the choice made for me due to my previous life? By this I mean that maybe your next life could be prejudged on how you live this life, or existence.

So then, is it pre-made karma or a judgement from a higher force or being? Nonetheless, those of you that are born healthy and well should be as grateful as I am. Those of you that are not, please continue reading and a reason and answer to this and all the questions above will emerge.

An Example of Our Creation

Imagine your father building a robot, the robot being you. As with any computer system he has built a program into the system which will protect you from viruses. These viruses are life's temptations.

There are secret codes, which, once discovered, will open up and allow access to a higher level of intelligence for you; these codes are the codes of life. These codes are relayed to us by the spiritual prophets and many righteous and wise individuals.

By ignoring them, we lose the ability to access and break the code; this will leave us in a frozen state, unable to move forward, therefore creating frustrations and anger in the search for answers to our questions.

How do we access the codes?

The code is to have faith in a higher spiritual presence which will in-turn humble you and make you pure in heart, allowing you to understand and differentiate between good and evil, by doing this, it opens parts of the brain which then release positive endorphins into your thought patterns. The more you focus on doing what is right the more powerful you can become, allowing you to do things beyond the natural understanding of our science.

The negative element of this power is other people. We are all connected; therefore other people's beliefs will interrupt and diminish your powers, if they do not believe in you. This is like your being a mobile phone; if it is in a negative area your reception is bad to the point it will not work at all. We can elaborate by saying at present it is like having a mobile phone in an era before satellites; you see the power is there; it only needs you to believe in it and learning what is required to release it, to make it work.

With the belief of others, it would be like having thousands of satellites made available to you all at once, enhancing your powers ten fold, this is where miracles begin and all is possible.

One thing I need to make clear, you cannot fake belief, as true faith is a power source.

Another example of creation is this. Take for instance a mountain, when you look at this colossal structure it is sometimes hard to comprehend how this has come to be, yet due to the earths creative volcanic and turbulent eruptions such a creation can exist, with its shape, size and scars one can recognise its being, this is classed as a material growth, the same applies to a spiritual growth, what separates the two are emotions, as emotions are as great, if not greater an energy than the movements of the universe.

Is it destined for a person to have a child?

No – it is our free will to have a child, a person is alone to make their own choices in life.

The Childs family is subsequently assessed spiritually by the natural selection of their subsequent existences; a soul/conscience will then merge into the body of that child. This will take place when the child has acknowledged its surroundings; what it remembers.

This can be envisaged by understanding nature and wildlife. For example, an octopus has thousands of offspring, as we have thousands of sperm. Once the offspring are born, most of them are eaten, and the result is food for other sea life, which makes you question why a higher power, be it God, should send life only to be destroyed within minutes, or days, of its birth. This would have no relevance for a soul, the only reason and justification for this is if a child dies, it can only be a test or stepping stone for mankind; it would open feelings within you that could only have been awoken by this extreme, by divining you or pushing you deeper into darkness, this could allow you to embrace, or push, your spiritual beliefs away; that choice in life is also and only YOURS.

Every child born brings into the world either salvation or slaughter.

Consequences of having a child

Be aware those who choose to have children; spiritually these souls are always connected to you, just as a branch to a tree. If the child becomes bad, all of its negativity affects you! This will unbalance any positive areas of your life you try to build; hence your life will be full of instability. To protect yourself against this, you 'must' at all costs educate your child to a righteous path, allowing your child to understand all the elements within this book and to understand the wisdom of a higher holy power, and world messengers of peace, Jesus, and many prophets, right from wrong, also teach your child to read sacred scriptures as a guide, thereupon the choice is theirs, as long as you have guided them and made the choice available to them, by doing this, you leave negativity in their hands.

Many children ask why they should pay for the sins of their parents, this is not so, you are reborn into your next existence 'be it this one' due to your own past actions in a past existence, it's the combination of you and your parents previous lives which has brought you together in this one, you yourselves have and always are in control of your future selves.

Many of us, once married with children, wish to go out sometime and leave the child with a babysitter.

'Beware'! You may know the babysitter really well and have full trust in this person, but choose carefully. I cannot stress enough the danger of this process. Remember, the child knows nothing of life, regarding what is normal, right or wrong. Many of you are none the wiser as to what the babysitter gets up to with your child, be aware, no matter whom it is, this is not their child and so they can be less reserved towards the treatment of this child. Take into account the age of the babysitter, family or friend. Using family members as babysitters, who you believe to be trust worthier, can lead to misjudgement, so do not be fooled.

Be wise, if the child is old enough to speak, after the babysitter has gone, ask your child what they did, try to ask as many questions as possible, probing every possible angle to do with violence, sexual abuse, shouting etc. This should be carried out in a way that does not traumatise the child. The child may have experienced something which it believes was normal but once heard by you turns out to be the complete opposite.

You may be saying to yourself 'this person is well overreacting; it is your right to think what you want. Please go ahead and question what you have read, the child is yours. All I ask from you is to keep an open mind; no one can trust another person like oneself. You may think you know that person but no one can say that, you are only fooling yourself, do not leave it until it is too late.

Is it not better to have two babysitters of equal respect and trust so they can both keep an eye on each other?

CHILD DEATH

Once you reach an understanding of life's true purpose and meaning, when a child is taken, it will then and only then be recognised as a gift to that soul from God/benevolent and enlightened conscience. (Any evil that befalls you is a cleansing of the soul) 'This action opens areas of the mind which could only happen by this kind of emotional trauma'. If the child is at the age of consciousness, (to make conscious decisions), it would mean that the only purpose that child was here was to enlighten the parents and surrounding members. The child would have been an old soul who was very spiritual in his/her previous existence.

Therefore, God is well pleased with it, taking the child before it becomes infected (corrupted) by society, this action will allow the soul to enter a final stage of material existence.

If the child was not of consciousness then it had the same purpose in enlightening you but was not a past soul.

Your anger at the mere suggestion that this is a gift is due to the fact that you must not only see this child as an earthbound being created by you, recognise it as a separate entity/soul; you are the vessel required for its transportation into this life.

For all of you that grieve, remember to always love those

around you every minute of every day, as you do not know how long their time here on Earth is for; as they are your earthly connections.

If they are your children, then educate them well, with a spiritual upbringing, as that child is like a crop, if it is carefully nurtured you shall yield a bumper harvest, a joy which will last for you now and for eternity. If you lead your life righteously nobody dies, they await you, let the dead bury the dead. 'This is a fact'. **Believe.**

ABORTION

To be wise – if you make love to a woman you must take the risk value upon yourself; the risk is not only the protection against transmitted diseases but understanding that you play with the life and death of a creation.

If you make a mistake by lack of protection and then decide to abort, this will be a sin/negative, as 'you' were responsible for your mistake. For you to then redeem yourself spiritually you must take responsibility for the child which you create. Life is not to be played with in the manner of ordering too much food therefore throwing the remainder away. If you have taken full protection and still have a pregnancy it would still be classed as a sin to abort, as you know that each time you make love there is always a chance of this happening.

To fully protect yourself from sin/creating negative energies to befall you, would be to make love only to the partner you believe you want to be the mother of your children.

To question the reasoning behind this is simple; your lust is earthbound and just another stepping-stone to the other temptations thrown in your way for evil to laugh at you when you fall.

This will be one of the greatest obstacles the weak flesh has to battle against.

If you have been raped, spiritually it should not be judged as a sin/negative element for you to terminate the 'precursor' of a birth, but remember, the earthly energies created by the unborn process will grow and will always be with you, it can become part of your earthly presence, a force which can be enhanced and called upon to weaken or strengthen your divinity, your pursue of good and evil.

Testing on embryos

An embryo should at all times be recognised and respected as life, testing for the greater purpose of life can create a positive and negative balance, if testing is done for inappropriate scientific experimentation it is a sin/negative. The action taken towards the embryo depending on how it was used will leave behind the relevant energy which will take effect on earth. If it is negative, you create negativity for all mankind. The death of any living thing creates negativity.

GROWING UP

We are born with the mind of an angel or like an empty programme of a computer, and now its time to program that chip.

Thought, intelligence, evil, good and wisdom are some of the many things we learn. This starts with your family, I do not just mean your parents, even though they are your first predominant programmers, but your grandparents, uncles, aunts etc, also play a major part.

As you begin to speak, walk and talk, a pattern emerges and one can see and attribute to what side of the family you have taken after, each blaming the other for the bad and praising oneself for the good. At this child stage your mind is not your own, it copies its surroundings, as in the phrase "you are what you eat". In this case, you are what you see! Harry Enfield portrays, (in his comedy series), a sketch called 'The Slobs'. It is scary to its reality of this type of family, and to which can be seen as a parasite to mankind as mankind is a parasite to its environment. Some are born with genetic disturbances, which are not a fault on either side, but I am just referring to what mainstream calls "normality" or more commonly "accepted".

You can always spot the "parasite" before they start school: - unwashed, smelly, shaven head, bruising. You see this child and can only feel sorry. Only counselling and preferably being taken away from their current family environment could help, but more often than not this would be totally unacceptable. "There is nothing wrong with the way we bring up our kids mate" the child's parents would say.

Those of us who are of good nature would dread having our children go to the same school as these but cannot afford to pay for a private school. Therefore we have a crazed psychopathic child putting a virus into our child's programming and when they come home, having to fight to remove that virus. You see these "slobs" are proud of being what they are and can not envisage being any other way, as a talking pre-programmed computer would say 'there is nothing wrong with me, this is the way I was programmed'. Easy solution for a computer, you just re-program it; not so easy with a human with a will of its own.

Ask yourself why "you" are the way you are, if you cause harm to anyone or anything please take a step back and question your reasons, help mankind by helping yourself.

Is there a way to avoid this virus? As an idea, our children would be safer educated in the same way the elder of us are by attending further education courses. There are training programs for any subject which can be followed and passed onto our children by the parents, with the bonus of re-educating ones self. I can understand that many of the parents have not got the time due to having to work, but if the parents could build up a selected friend-base, they could all contribute. With sponsorship from the government they could create individual private play schools. We could also delegate some of the parents who have fewer work obligations to help with the education and balance it out with the rest of them.

Another possible solution is virtual education, using television and computers. There education can be regulated by regular exams. The youth's friend base can be accumulated by interaction via the site.

(The sensible way is to re-educate humanity).

SECONDARY SCHOOL, mind of a juvenile

There was a group of about five or six school boys (and some others who would join in on odd occasions). They would all be together as a group, chat and contemplate what to do.

Well, there was this other boy who used to sit on this little wall every playtime; he was one or two years above the others. He used to carry this satchel with him everywhere and used to place it behind his legs as he sat on the small wall used as seats by the pupils.

He would sit there reading a book that was placed high in front of his face. Now, the boys got to learn that if you bumped into this person at any time while he was in this position he would go crazy and end up punching or kicking you, so they came up with what they called 'our sacrifice' game.

They were in their third year of school at this time, so the obvious sacrifices were, of course, the first year boys. The game was played as follows. At playtime, while the boy with a dubious name was in position, they would march back and forwards in front of him with their left hands over their noses and the right hand going backwards and forward as if playing a trumpet and making trumpet noises. They did this because the boy had a big nose and they knew this would irritate him more, they would also chant an antonym of his name, as this would be the opposite meaning to his surname.

Once they saw that he was really angry to a point of eruption, they would then choose their victim. They would start their hunt to stalk a first year boy whilst they would be in the middle of their regular playtime football matches, totally unaware of the third year boy's presence. The older boys would surround and pounce, one on each arm and one on each leg so there was no getting away. They would then carry him head first towards the so designated beast, chanting, 'sacrifice, sacrifice, sacrifice' increasing in volume the closer they got. The first year boy would be struggling to get away, but to no avail, then when they were two feet from the "beast" they would hurl the victim onto him and watch the carnage as the boy was punched and kicked a multitude of times, mission accomplished, till the next time.

This sad but true story gives you an insight into the minds of adolescents to which we pray that in the future we can somehow re-educate our thought process so that, one day, the pain caused to many for the amusement of others can be eradicated once and for all.

Mankind should not be recognised as mature and rational thinkers until they reach the age of twenty-six.

Questions & answers –

Why can't I be wise before the age of 26?

Gaining wisdom is a process of life's experiences, including a level of maturity the body and mind naturally begin to form at this age.

CAREER

What do you want to do with your life? Where do you want to go? You may not know. There are many things passing through your mind but you are possibly still not sure. Your teachers are giving you advice. Your parents are doing the same; some with quite a lot of pressure and some who believe in you to make up your own mind. As a partner may say "give the child some space darling, they'll soon come to the right decision".

Many times this is not the case; the teenager would probably like to do something which would outrage the parents to which the parents will in no way help with this irresponsible decision 'STOP' and think? One must become their child and not have distanced themselves along the way from the child they used to be. Help them by delving deeper into what your child has chosen. Do your homework; show the pluses and downfalls of their career prospects.

The teenager does not have the same mental wisdom as yourself and so you, 'the adult' must rise above it and use the wisdom you have to evaluate the situation.

Also one must not shout at your child for the decision they have come to. Try to rationalise with them; once you start to shout it puts your child into a defence mode, they in return, will shout, whereupon the result would have been a stressed noise.

Patience is a virtue, use it, as difficult as it may be, you are the adult!

Master your emotions by controlling them rather than allowing your emotions to control you.

WORK

Your choice of work is also important to your life's balance of positive and negative, being: - If you are in sales you should not relay a falsehood upon your client. The goods you sell must be recognised as goods you would consider buying yourself.

If you are in the financial business you must not offer a financial package which will render the customer at a loss without their secured understanding and knowledge. Anything sold by the play of a word 'to make it sound better than it is', or to mislead, is a sin. Always consider if your position creates upset to the customer. If it does, avoid it as it will unbalance your present and future.

Those who are in a position which saves lives are in a blessed place. Those in the medical profession, police, firemen etc. should be seen by governments/society as the greatest of beings but only if deserving. If you decide to take up one of these positions you must take the job by the full understanding and implications of what it entails.

As an example, to enter the medical profession an individual should be properly vetted, not only for their intelligence but more importantly, for their moral beliefs. You are in a position of trust.

In the above positions, and over a period of time, many feel it is necessary to develop a way to disconnect. It is not necessary; you must never disconnect yourself for whatever means you may think, by doing this you render your heart cold; if you feel you must, then this is not the job for you.

You must always, and at all times, place yourself in the strangers place or even acknowledge them as a loved one/nearest and dearest, as only then will you receive the blessing and the enlightenment you justly deserve.

Forbear to do this can place you in the realms of darkness and become a sin.

The world should then acknowledge and reward the deserving ones with just dividends for they are the givers of life not the media, entertainers or sport.

WHAT IS LOVE & The glamour model

Love is an emotion that can only be felt but never fully explained.

What is Love?

There are so many games which are played amongst couples today as to what is perceived as normal. The lack of trust is always there and questions are asked of each other such as: -

Where did you go after work?

Who with?

Why did you have to work late?

Without going too deep into these games let me get straight to the point. You will instantly know whether or not it is true love you have found.

Areas to look out for if it is NOT true love are: -

You want to change them.

After sex, you push them away due to a decrease of emotions.

When they call or text you, it is annoying.

Going to see them is a chore.

You miss clubbing.

You think of how your ex is doing etc.

When it IS true love: -

You think of them constantly.

When you are out shopping you think of buying them things.

After lovemaking you want to hold them and never let go which gives a sense of happiness and security with an overwhelming protective nature.

You put your partner on a pedestal above all others and you will feel secure in the belief that there is only you and no others in their lives.

A partner should be viewed in this way: - If you decide to build your own house, make sure the foundation to it is strong, as if it is not, in time your house will tumble, your partner is the foundation, and the house is your future.

There was this television show where a man's girlfriend wanted to become a glamour model but the boyfriend didn't want her to. She said she would be loyal and that he should trust her, as it was a career move for her and that was all. He said he did not want his woman to show off her body to all and sundry and that he would find it hard to trust her in those surroundings. The reality of it would be that if she really loved him, she would feel the hurt she was causing him by being in that role and her heart would not allow her to do it. Some woman would then say, if he loved me he would put the hurt he feels aside and let me do it.

Taking it to its extreme would be like your partner saying they want to star in porn films but they do not make love to the actors, as it is only you they love. If you cannot understand the irony of that then you are naïve and very foolish.

Why do the women of today no longer respect themselves?

Due to their own selfishness and lust, fuelled by alcohol, they have become harlots. They cut a groove into the headboard for each male they sleep with and feel proud.

Why then does a man degrade himself by taking one of these women as a wife when he knows how much depravity she has embraced and indulged in, and the same applies for the man.

For a person to understand this kind of emotion, imagine what goes on whilst making love and picture the woman you are about to marry who has allowed this to be done to her; not once, or even five times, but depending on age, a multitude.

At times how can one ask for respect when one does not respect oneself?

With either sex, if you were to ever meet the one that you love, only then will you feel guilt about your shameful past, a feeling of being unclean.

A man at that level of understanding sees himself as the user, using the woman as a vessel of his depravity; the woman is fooled into believing she is the user but results in only allowing herself to be abused.

In a perfect world would you not love to meet one who has saved themselves for true love, to marry for true love, to know that no other has abused the object of your adoration?

PROSTITUTION, and how the positive/negative elements apply

You can chose to be what you want in this world, but take heed, due to your chosen path you are the one responsible for the emotional hurt placed on loved ones, family, friends and lovers.

To understand the emotional negativity you release you must place yourself in your parent's position. Would you like to see your daughter doing this?

Prostitution on an earthly sense can be regarded for these reasons: - If there are males or females which strive for sex and cannot satisfy their hunger for this, then your chosen trade can be the release valve for their frustration. Without you, these people may fall to temptation and find a deeper depravity, they may rape or abuse. This should be governed and legalised with a Law that protects you.

The clients should give full identification for records to be kept, and the Law should prosecute if their identification is leaked to any other than the Law. All safety requirements should be used to protect both parties.

What you should not do once you decide to be a prostitute: – you must not have a loving partner. If you have one who agrees and wants you to do this without emotional attachment then this may be possible. You must be without parents or children as even if you kept this a secret from them, knowing how they would feel if they knew, is still a collective negative element which will inevitably cause you harm.

Choosing this career, even with good intentions, would create a negative energy in your life, which will automatically take you in a negative direction. If you were to choose to marry; your partner would also be of a negative element, as the Holy Spirit/positive elements in life would not allow a righteous person to stray into your path.

If this is your chosen path, protection must be used at all times, as it is known that a sexual disease can kill. If you still decide against protection, spiritually you are acknowledged as a murderer, reaping all the negativity it befalls.

Pornography

Pornography is of no good intention. Yes, it can be said that this is also a sexual release, but it has more of a negative effect on humanity than good. It influences the weakness of humanity to a higher level of depravity. This should be stopped along with all negative viewing and interaction via television, music and paperback, - all media. Remember we are all recognised as Gods children, meaning being born gifted with pure angelical qualities, respect yourself and keep those qualities for the world to admire and follow.

STRAYING FROM YOUR PARTNER
Adultery

If you win a paradise island sculptured to your specification with all the amenities you wish for, even though there are other islands near by nice to look at and would be nice to visit, why would you ever consider swapping? Meaning if your partner has everything you crave, then in some circumstances, it can be recognised as a natural action for you to look at passing beauty, but yours has that and more, so there will never be any need to swap or stray. To do so is a betrayal to yourself and to your partner.

Also with so many sexual diseases abundant, you not only betray your partner but also put their life at peril for your own selfish cravings. Is this the way to treat the one you love, to compromise their life? And if you have children, you selfishly risk the loss of their mother.

The natural elements of life would categorise this as manslaughter and this should be how the law should recognise it. If you feel the need to stray then separate, at least have the decency to leave your family in safety and eventual peace to begin a new life.

Spiritually – Woes are they who have done this as the path you have chosen to go down has been carved by the devil/negativity that beckons and awaits you with a wink and smirk.

A woman is under the illusion that she as an individual stands out above all women when she gets the attention of many men; this is a grave mistake. As an example, there was a survey done where a presenter of a show took an average male into the high street, stopped and asked thirty individual women if they would allow this man to take them away at that moment and sleep with him. All the women said no, yet the same was done using a woman and the outcome was that all thirty men approached said yes. I believe that this would go to prove the above. Yet the realities are that, until the moral attitude and thought of either sex are changed, then either will continue to chase their frills and conquests both for the purpose of quenching there insecurities and depravities.

MARRIAGE

To make a vow in the name of God and break it is a sin. One must truly love the other to even contemplate making that vow.

Marriages made for other reasons such as: – money, comfort, loneliness and selfishness, should just live together. The laws of the land should still apply for both parties if they were to separate, they split everything they own as a couple. In straightforward cases, both share custody of any children.

Society has separated the world by race, colour, creed and position. Try to put this aside when choosing a partner, as when true love exists, none of these things would matter. The race culture has been so deeply imbedded that it will be hard for you to disconnect yourself without true love. Therefore, if you want your happiness to last, to marry for love is the only way; any other reason will leave you with sadness and longing.

SPIRITUALITY OF MARRIAGE

If your partner is not righteous, to get married is a hindrance. The reason is that this will end up in chaining yourself to earthly things; it will lead to buying property, a higher paid steady job, shackling you to the necessity of money which will take away your freedom and place you in the realms of ignorant slavery. You see, everything the earth has taught you to crave is a way of enslaving you, and spiritual death. Once you wallow in earthly treasures, in the spiritual realm you are recognised as a negative element, as all you would have accomplished is unwillingly added debauchery for your offspring and mankind to sink deeper into.

Questions & answers –

The man who quoted 'best to have loved and lost than never to have loved at all' is a fool -

No, he had divine insight. To love and lose in an earthbound way is very painful, but once you lead a righteous life you never lose any love, your love will come with you when you pass on and last forever, therefore for you to know the experience of true love is a gift, as if you don't, you cant take that with you. It is like the love of a parent, once experienced it stays with you as long as you live.

Anything of exuberance gained from life passes with you only if your faith in God (to live your life for others) is real. If not, then make the most of what you have, as due to your choices in life, when it has gone it has gone forever.

My father tells me to marry for comfort, as love is a fad.

Everyone these days search so hard to find a partner to give them comfort in life rather than love and then end up doing themselves the greatest injustice ever known, as love is the greatest of all life's gifts which is taken with you and kept for eternity. As a tiny example, in life, do you remember the love of a parent, the love of a pet, and truly heart pounding emotional events? When you are truly in love these emotions never fade.

My girlfriend wants me to be a hard man, should I go along.

For your girlfriend to want to change you in anyway means she does not love you. You are perfect the way you are in the eyes of your correct partner. Your girlfriend will only help to corrupt you and lead you towards a road filled with self destruction.

Should I marry my partner?

If you need to ask then you are not ready to marry them. Question your need to ask. For your married life to go smoothly you must marry for 'LOVE' and only love, this 'must' be true, as you make a vow to God and build a foundation for the future.

If this is broken or untrue it will be a sin and a marriage filled with instability.

DRUGS

A poem I wrote as a teenager -

> *No sex, no drugs, no porno, no thugs, no little fu....g moron with nobody to love.*
> *I blame my mother, my sister, my social workers brother, anybody else but ME.*

Narcotics, be it drugs or alcohol, these are taken by the weak, those who have lost their way, those who have let society be their only world and only existence, (their conqueror), those of a closed mind who have no further belief, not even in themselves, having nothing else to live for.

You have let the rich man destroy you; you have let the pompous hypocrite you loathe destroy you. Is your life really worth so little? Are you truly the pathetic looser they have labelled you as?

You have a soul and if you allow that soul to believe in God/a greater existence beyond this one, and follow a righteous path, then you are above any person, whether they are of title or of Gold. Throw their poisons away and live, as life is such a precious gift.

If you had the choice to live life in a cave, would you not like some light? So do not let others take away that light. Drugs will leave you in the darkness.

Once you are in control of your own emotions with a righteous nature, then a tipple of alcohol can in some circumstances be a pleasure; illegal drugs can never be, as these are tainted with the blood of the innocent and affect the mind in many hidden ways.

Mankind have conditioned themselves to believe the only way to wind down and have fun is to consume large amounts of alcohol. Society has also brainwashed you to encourage this.

The young man uses alcohol as a symbol of being a "hard man", believing it shows their friends how manly they are.

They also compete to how much they can consume; believing the more they can consume the more of a "man" they are.

Oh, how weak minded and sad those people really are! All the hard work you have done to collate your money so you can squander on a liquid which not only helps deplete your mental state but also reduces your libido and destroys your health.

Then it is used as an excuse for your idiotic and harmful behaviour towards others, as if you cannot remember, we all know you DO remember!! This only released your inhibitions to portray the restrained you. Ask yourself, is this something a sane and sensible person would do? You are the dangerous parasite that puts the rest of mankind in fear of walking the streets at night, the elderly who fear wandering out of their own homes. How proud you must feel to create such misery, as if it was to happen to someone you know, then, you are the first to condemn.

Humanity should not be lenient on these addicts; this is a weakness not an addiction. It is a selfish indulgence and the majority of the time it was an individual's choice to take the drug.

Many of you have gone through a spell of stopping and have succeeded but yet you decided to go back on it. This only goes to prove that you do have the willpower to stop. It is you and you alone, who takes the decision not to; with the understanding of what damage and pain it causes not only to you but all that are connected to you, and to the drug. Therefore the world should see you for what you really are; a criminal, due to the money given for them destroys life, just so you can satisfy yours. You help the dealers distribute evil all around the globe and when you no longer can subsidise the cost of your indulgence, you steal, maim and kill, not just strangers but even your nearest and dearest. You are the nocturnal, a parasite who sleeps during the day and feeds at night, one who has caused themselves to suffer with paranoia, depression and schizophrenia just because you don't want to say no.

What is the cure?

Repent and find God/righteousness, change your ways and do good deeds which will help you master you own emotions. 'YOU' are the cure.

Questions & answers –

My friends are taking drugs, should I join in to be one of the crew.

You must know that drugs will physically destroy your body and mind in some way. Spiritually it can steal your soul. So then, if I was one of those friends and asked you to jump off a building with me to be part of a crew, 'would you'? Is your life worth so little; I am sure you are better than that. Stay clear of these people because with friends like these who needs enemies. They have lost their way, if you can't stop them then leave them.

THE BODY

For mankind to find enlightenment and clear the mind he must purify the body. Simply by having a healthy balanced diet and a simple fitness program can purify the body and the soul. This is a must for all who take their lives seriously. This will allow positive elements to enter the body and release all the negative toxins/elements, be it digested or life's stresses.

An example of how it works; imagine plying the body with pills, alcohol, smoke etc; the liver will get clogged and collapse. Another example is to leave your rubbish in a pile for ages; it will eventually start to stink, create bacteria, worms and will attract rats.

To explain, the body has all this food in it which needs cleaning/distributing, the good food passed around the body and the bad passed out or the effects will be as stated.

To have the belief of a 'just' higher force than yourself, be it God or any other 'just' and connected belief, will have the same effect on your spiritual being as what the immune systems effect on the body, as without your immune system your body will be open to all the natural worlds elements/germs, eventually break down and die.

The world and all it contains should also be envisaged as our body parts, by you then taking the action to fix a negative or problem area is like a Doctor doing the same to your body. The world is your body and you are its Doctor.

HOMOSEXUALITY and the spiritual laws

Being gay should be recognised as a personal sexual preference and should not be forced upon society as a natural act as monogamy is understood to be.

The Law should allow gays to marry if true love is expressed but through a government ceremony, not a religious one in respect of the fact that the Bible does not condone this. However, true love is greater than what is accepted by religious doctrines.

Gay adoption

Should gays be allowed to adopt? A morally justified society should not allow this; the reason being is that a child has no choice, so it is up to its elders and the wiser of us to give the child the opportunity to begin life in the most natural and stable surroundings. The mere suggestion of trying to justify a gay adoption is ludicrous and hypocritical if the world is to try and teach correctness to its future offspring.

If you take the theory of evolution, just the basic facts, then a woman is created and formed to have semen injected by a male penis into her womb to create a child and give birth. A person's bottom is for excreting bodily waste. Anything in between these facts is a society made fetish, a lustful pleasure, and should be kept as a personal preference.

This should not be about religion, politics or sex; the main and only importance here should be the welfare of the child. What we must try to comprehend is that a child does not, and cannot define or understand its surroundings; you must understand that these children have already been through hardship; therefore, we have to use common sense and human morality. To reiterate, we must think only of the child's welfare and not of oneself, or how this affects you on a personal level, which can wrongly influence the decision you make.

The child should be placed into what society recognises as being a normal upbringing, what we understand as normal/black and white. Normality is a family group consisting of a man and a woman, the child's first teachers are the parents from which it gains its knowledge and understanding of the world around it.

This child should, by no means be put, (without sounding prejudice or discriminative), into any family unit consisting of anything other than the above stated.

Please do not allow your sexual orientation to diminish the fact of responsibility to society. If the world were gay, would you choose to allow your own child to be brought up by straight people? This is not a battle to defend your sexuality, it is about a human being, and as any psychologist would tell you, a child should be given the chance to experience life as it should be, then when it has reached the age of consent, have the right to make their own decisions and choices. If the child is put with a gay couple, it can introduce elements of confusion into their life and may allow their mind to adopt a non-conformist upbringing which could affect their future and encourage the child to stray and experiment from their original sexual orientation.

Gay priests

Leave the priesthood, do not ridicule your faith owing to your selfish sexual needs or, (shall we say), your own twist of religion. If you are going to practice your religion, as so "preached", then you become hypocritical.

Priests should not be forced to be celibate. It can be of greater help for a priest to have a life like any other and teach the rest of us how a righteous life and children's upbringing should be.

If one wishes to be a holy man and is then told they cannot because man has forced a rule upon them, it is a sin/wrong doing. There should not be 'any' reason to stop a person from doing good.

No one, for no reason should be stopped from using the sacraments of God if they should so choose to have them: – christening, Holy Communion etc.

To remain celibate should remain the free will of the priest, whether male or female.

RACISM

There was a program about an Asian sheik travelling in Glasgow to where he was born, meeting and speaking to people to ask their views about multicultural inhabitants, to which the reply was; as always, society's racist element will always be among us.

He was trying to show the racism aimed towards him just because of wearing a turban. Then I ask you, if this man truly believed in trying to make others understand his plight, shouldn't he have taken it upon himself to prove he is willing to put an end to segregation by removing his turban and taking the first step to becoming part of the society in which he lives?

If a white man walks into a black neighbourhood it is enough for particular individuals to negatively react, but if he was to shave his head and mark his skin with skinhead propaganda does this not make him an enemy of himself, a provoker of anger and violence and the initiator of what he wants to curb?

Whether you go round branding a religion, an organisation or whatever is of importance to you, one must not force it upon others. One must recognise the anger in which he incites within those of little understanding and do anything that is necessary to keep the peace and walk in the footsteps of your God, your faith and your belief which all amounts to peace, love and understanding.

Those whom you are trying to convert have the same beliefs in their cultural lifestyle as you have in 'your' faith. The difference lies in who has the purest heart in taking the first steps to make a change as a start with the means to accomplishing an end, the beginning of a one 'US' not I.

ARE WE FREE?

Earth has brainwashed the human race in believing so, therefore we have the illusion of freedom. To be truly free one must let go of this materialistic world and work towards what is truly awaiting you outside of this realm and to understand and follow a moral way of life.

The society we live in has laid many traps. They have put out bate for you to bite. This may sound shocking and outrageous yet it is so, – Money, property, fame, self esteem; one is lead to believe that an intelligent person is one who has achieved the so mentioned. 'This is not so', all you have unwittingly become is a caged animal, controlled by a very sophisticated and intelligent/scrupulous order. Also at this present moment in 'time' to have a family and bring a child into the world entraps you by allowing this to be your main area of thought; as one would need to make enough money to look after the child. Can you see the connection, you may now be thinking 'yes but that's life and we have to live it so' 'DO YOU?

There is another existence outside this false reality and 'THAT' is life, not this, the difficulty lays in detaching ones self from a fabricated belief, to reach that understanding is only then recognised as true 'intelligence'.

As another example – **Desert Island** – Imagine being shipwrecked and you wake up on a deserted island. All the parcels containing money, precious jewels and designer ware are washed ashore; now ask yourself, what use they are to you on the island. What knowledge do we have to truly survive on our own? How do we purify the water to drink, or make fire, or clothe ourselves against the weather? How to build some kind of shelter, self medication encase of injury? The majority of us would die in a very short period of time, and that's the way our world wants it kept; for mankind to rely on governments/big brother for their survival 'or die'… This is also why we are not taught to be self-sufficient in schools. "So go out there and work your finger to the bone for the pieces of paper you're told your life is truly worth". Think.

THE RICH AND FAMOUS

Those who are in the public eye were possibly souls who were quite spiritual in their previous existence. They did try to understand and question life and, in the process, helped others; yet they did not reach their goal. They believed they would march into hell for a heavenly course. Their wish was granted and now they undertake that task in this lifetime, God has given you a destiny.

Your destiny is to be famous and worldly recognised, because to be in this position stands you on the edge of hell, (eternal peace or destruction), containing all its temptations and desires.

By reading this you now know your goal. You must be strong, as you are the messenger of God/peace; it will be recognised above all life as the sacrifice of leaving all your possessions for your faith. You are a beacon for the whole world; you will be a light in the depths of darkness, and for your sacrifice of your riches to become a servant to the weak, poor and needy.

Your reward would be in the realms of sainthood, as it is your actions which will change the hearts and minds of mankind, eternal happiness will be your gift. Do not fear letting go of your possessions, as you do it for the Divine good of humanity.

You will have the protection of the heavenly father 'the greatest protection and power of all'. You will be fed, clothed and have all you require by they who will love you, as there will be many. You will never go without, and all this will be yours without money. BELIEVE!!! And be that change the world is waiting for.

Wealth & happiness

Once you are one with the power of God/positive energy, the force gained from this will act as a protection from harm and negative elements. You can then achieve happiness on earth as happiness is within us all. It is a simple thought process, a way of mind, not a way of materialistic happiness and values.

It is not what one profits in a lifetime, it is what you achieve. Wealth is gained by those you have converted to righteousness.

And he said unto them, go ye into all the world, and preach the gospel to every creature. (Mark 16:15)

Mind set

You must let go of all your current earthly values, such as; achieving success, gaining power of any kind, material richness. You must be strong and ignore all those around you who temp you towards these earthly things for they are blind and lobotomised by the world. You must treat every life the way you wish to be treated by placing every action in that category. You are here to serve not to be served and most importantly to convert all negative elements to positive/all evil to good.

To begin, this will be very difficult but will become as simple a way of life as prior. The only difference is that a great reward awaits you beyond your greatest wish. **BELIEVE**.

Just look at history, all those prophets and saints before did just that. Their lives where engulfed with scorn and hardship, and from who; other human beings, 'YOU'. Yet now they are worshiped by the same, so please do not let man/others cloud your true purpose. Yet, just like a teenager fuelled on alcohol who denies remembering the devastation they caused under the influence, the rich person and nobility will do the same with this knowledge and what they have just read, whilst fuelled on money.

THE MEDIA

Television and paparazzi have the most influence on mankind therefore, spiritually everything negative which results from the Media will be returned to them. This applies to all employees. If one knows of a wrong in what they do, or help do, or even contribute to doing, one must remove oneself from it.

The media deny this but the evidence is obvious. If you go and watch a gangster film you come out admiring them and imagine yourself as one. If you see a good deeds film you come out imagining yourself and wanting to become a good doer. The human mind is weak and those who are earthly bound are the most susceptible.

The same applies with the newspapers. If someone is suspected of a murder they did not commit, but assumptions are made as to their guilt, the majority of the population will follow suit. They have been misguided and swayed into reaching their belief. Even though you may think they are not guilty, a constant barrage of negative assumptions on the mind will effect your decision either way.

The media is to be used as a guide not a full gone conclusion. Many times what you see, read and hear is a skilled form of mind control/propaganda, be wise.

THE RICH DESTROYERS

The rich who teach and subsequently brainwash their offspring to believe that money is greater than life itself due to their self loathing and ignorance of not believing in anything outside of the earth, has created their pomposity, and money has become an addiction, as a heroin addict to narcotics, therefore has spread and infected the whole world and leads us all to spiritual destruction. Observe the rich for what they truly are, the destructors of not only the human race, but of life itself.

WORLD NEWS

A relic was partially destroyed by fire. The media had made this event to be of such importance and it was shown many times. Money was sponsored so quickly by businesses etc and, in no time, hundreds of thousands was accumulated for the relic's restoration. If only mankind could direct that kind of emotion into helping the Third World or others closer to home in need, this world would soon be a better place. Yet this story shows how the human race has lost its way.

WHY MONEY?

At one stage the world managed to survive for a thousand years without war and lived and bartered by an exchange of skills and what they grew or owned.

Someone, somewhere, sometime, in a high position of power came to the idea that by creating money would enslave the world's population in a more humane manner without the population realising the veil which has been pulled over their eyes. As time went on, there were many different ways those in power had created many means in gaining money and reasons why the people had to get it for their own survival. This had made those creators very powerful by turning mankind into tax-paying zombies.

Also the education process had to be changed so as not to allow us too much self-reliance, gadgets keep us entertained - (televisions and computers being some of its greatest distractions) - catapulting us into the wrong direction, which was right for them.

So a person's life revolves around the fact that we have a good enough education to get a well-paid job and be able to buy a home and start a family. To do this we now need to work so many hours of the day, be it for ourselves or for an employer. After our hard work we are herded like live stock into bars, clubs and pubs to drink ourselves into a stupor for those few days of freedom we have to ourselves and then pick ourselves back up to start all over again.

Alcohol and drugs are also one of the greatest distraction brought in by those of power to keep us in a zombie state, so not to realise the truth of what our government, (or if there are other forces which control government), have taken away our freedom by a blanket of dissolution. Many who have seen through this have tried to enlighten others but have been swiftly silenced.

The enslaving of man evolved due to those in power losing, or not being able to hold onto the power they had, as the way humanity lived made all equal, therefore leaving those in power no control over its population. Or the possibility in stumbling across technologies that man should be kept in the dark about. Did they learn of something beyond our capabilities, which, in return, informed those of how to control its surroundings? Or could it be as simple as mans inhumane genetic tendencies, which without a manner of control, humanity would resort to its beginning and behave in the same way as the animals in the wild, as we witness on a daily occurrence.

The purpose for man controlling man may have started out as good intensions but you can be certain that greed, selfishness and power soon overcome to then enslave humanity for the benefit of those who are now in control.

The suppressors have unwillingly unlocked the gates to an unknown spiritual reality which exists outside their comprehension.

STORY OF TWO BUILDINGS

I am about to tell you a story explaining the way in which those who call themselves, 'the world order' think, and how they use the people, 'their flock', with thousands of years knowledge in using skilful propaganda . Below is a chosen scenario of their thought processes and strategies. Based on past events.

Let us assume that two of the tallest buildings were constructed at a time when countries wanted to show their power. These buildings had just that purpose, which was achieved.

Many years' later, health and safety rules found the fire protective interior toxic and had to be changed, which would cost billions to structure and business. At this time, intelligence believed a certain country to be a threat to them and had heard that there would be an attack by that country on the buildings. Instead of stopping this from happening, their council decided to use this information to the countries favour and therefore allow the attack to take place. This would not only save them millions from the restructure of the buildings, including the insurance claim, but also give them the consent of the disillusioned public to strike a counter attack against that country, allowing the countries oil wealth as compensation for toppling a dictatorship for them, accomplishing a double bonus.

The loss of life would compensate for what they call the greater good!!! You see, they believe the countries money and power comes before a few lives.

To make money from your farm a proportion of your life stock must be sacrificed!!!!!... Many of you will find this hard to digest, if you then want to ignore it, do so, all I ask is that in future, do not just accept what the media tells you, as they control the media in more ways than they are currently controlling you.

I have a question for you, in the history of tall buildings, has there ever been an occasion where a tall structure has ever collapsed in a perfect line without it being controlled? In the search for an answer you will find it never has occurred.

Question if this could happen to one of the tallest buildings in the world, it could be recognised as a miracle, and then, what are the odds of it happening to two at the same time and place, including a third near by!

IRRESPONSIBLE ESTABLISHMENTS

The lack of manners within establishments such as the police and army is just an insult to the intelligence and morality of mankind. For us to move forward, any psychiatrist worth his grain would tell you that to rudely force and demoralise people rather then politely encourage them is just a step back to Neanderthal mentality that will only result in the cadet believing violence to be the way forward, resulting in sowing a seed of hate in the offenders character.

It is time to change the teaching processes of these establishments, redirecting them in how to engage with the public. If we are to be taught the law, which is supposed to be seen as a moral guide for us all, then its time to act in a morally correct manner. Allow man to respect and admire, rather than loath and hate your use of conduct. The establishments must stop viewing themselves as a law unto themselves, 'them and us', and start to become one with the public, so we can eventually start to work together as an upstanding society. Allow the courts to be courts of justice, not courts of law.

Police and hospitals run on a target basis. Soldiers give up their lives for whom? Common sense tells us if you offer someone money to sell something, many left to their own devises will lie and cheat to get it, with no moral ethics on the outcome of the person they had just sold it to, then why put targets on the Police? They should seek this employment for what it should stand for, to help others and not to put the innocent behind bars for the sole benefit for that officer to reach their target, get their bonus and in time a higher rank. This is total hypocrisy, the same goes for the hospitals, target, target, target, to a point in which some nurses have been jailed for allowing the elderly and most vulnerable to die to make room and have more beds for new patience, for the sole purpose of reaching their TARGET!!!!

So you want to become a soldier. Then go ahead and fight for your country, which by the way is not yours, just as much as if you were born on an aeroplane, it does not make the plane yours.

If thieves plan to come and steal that plane, why would you enrol to go and protect it with your life and the lives of your close friends and family? So then when it is all over and you're without limb, do you truly think the government give a damn about you?

For example, when they are in their command box giving the order for you and your comrades to be sent into a suicidal stand without your knowledge, 'acknowledged as', "acceptable collateral", at that moment, how much do you think they really care about YOU?

What about the Geneva Convention hypocrisy? When you are at war, in the minds of the soldiers, 'it is just that'!! Their fear and harsh mind numbing training conditions them to one belief, they are there to kill or be killed and the Geneva Convention is just a blanket to hide behind.

We have been given witness to the realities of this in the Iraqi war and countless others. When many of our "civilised" people go to protect the "uncivilised" nation and end up acting more barbaric than the opposition. All I ask is, 'wake up people', and smell the roses! Life may not be all what we are led to believe, the truth would blow our minds away, as I believe it is way beyond our comprehension.

War is not a game and should not be treated as one. When fear takes over, many lose all morality, and inevitably become inhumane. Humanity is not conditioned for or cannot understand the art of chivalry and honour for ones race (mankind). We are a weak species who needs to evolve tenfold to obtain the slightest comprehension of who and what we truly are. Something needs to be done to make those with sight see and those that hear listen; yet I believe it is too late for many.

Think rationally.

So we the people are forced to pay for road humps, speed cameras, police time and court costs, resulting in incarceration etcetera, etcetera, for the purpose of stopping the speeding motorist. All this creates is anger to the motorist, anger for the layman and adding to existing world chaos. As an example of a simple solution: - we already have satellite navigation built into cars with an existing computer onboard, hence the cars speed can be controlled by satellites. Each road has its speed limit; once a car is on that road and tries to go over the speed limit the onboard computer directed by the satellite can restrict it from doing so.

There are many practical solutions to life's problems being suppressed for the selfish purposes of others.

THE CURRENT FUTURE OF OUR PLANET

We have an elite group of powerful people; the technologies they have will become so advanced to a point when they will no longer need their flock, "mankind", as we are currently a necessity for their survival. We will become a hindrance to them and the planet. We will then need to be eradicated for their beliefs of a greater good. At that point they will create a new way of life with the collaboration of non terrestrial beings;

this will help distance the benevolent ones, as our world would then have chosen to become a negative element to the universe.

This can yet be changed if we the people can re-educate mankind to a spiritual awakening and for all of us to take responsibility in guiding our offspring in the ways of kindness and peace. Do not become your own worst enemy, as this is what the elite are, 'whether consciously or inadvertently', conditioning you to become.

To simplify the above, the world order use humanity, their flock, 'us', as a bartering system for an alien intelligence to protect the Earth from natural disasters that could put us into partial extinction.

DO WE HAVE A DESTINY – PRE-DESTINED

Yes we do have different possible destinies which can be altered by the way we approach them, i.e., our journey towards them. If on the way there we follow the good path and lead a righteous life, we will not lose our way and therefore receive the positive path. If not, an alternative destiny faces you, which is full of danger and instability.

We begin with a purpose, just like the cogs of a wheel, for example; - look at all the world's elements and how they interact. Each living thing and natural element has a purpose for the continuation of life. Then when we begin to understand and question our lives, the choices we make and take create our destiny.

What if my final destination is not a good one?

It does not matter if it is bad on this Earth plain/this existence. If you lead your life correctly, you are then guided by God/collective good energies; therefore, your reward awaits you.

Do not get bogged down by the world we live in, as you must concentrate on what is to follow in your afterlife/next existence.

WHAT DOES MY FUTURE YIELD

As a crime can be traced by the diagnostics of clues left behind at/or around the scene, also can your future be diagnosed by your past and present. Just as you carve your future path by what you do today. If you wrong a person, yet they forgive you, your penance, being the negative energy created by your action, will still need to be paid unless you understand this and try to balance it by a similar good/positive deed. The good deed will not eliminate your penance but once this has been served, thereafter awaits stability, and if the good deeds continue, so will the rewards for your deeds, as the positive actions will help balance both negative and positive. Some may never be able to resolve their bad deeds in a lifetime but may see the rewards in the afterlife/next existence.

Some may have a destiny that can reveal itself if ones eyes and mind are open. Your destiny cannot be changed but you can change the outcome before and after it has occurred, accumulating in a possible alternative destiny. If you cannot see your negativity, ask the wisdom of a righteous person, as just by looking at your appearance their wisdom heeded may be able to stop an inevitable outcome.

To explain this further, your destiny to become a fire-fighter is dictated by your previous existence. If you are a new life form your destiny has been sculpted due to the combined consciences of other life forms.

Your journey towards and following your destiny/chosen vocation is created in this existence, meaning, the actions you make in this life time affects the outcome before and after becoming a fire-fighter.

As an example to how the wise person recognises you: - when narcotics get into the blood your total appearance tells others of your vices, meaning: - when you see a drug addict he is quite easily noticed/recognised, which in the same manner, when negative elements grab hold of you your appearance to a righteous man will be apparent.

When at school, the pupils' quest is to be the centre of attention, to be respected, feared by males and idolised by the girls. To do this he begins to bully, to back talk and be rude to his teachers, accumulating in classroom fights, vandalism, smoking, and possible tattoos. Theses actions flow into outside criminal activities with the other school friends to which his attitude has attracted. This does reach the goal he was looking for at that particular time of his life. But then when he leaves school, all his antics, which have left him with a bad school record and no or low exam results, and no prospects for the future, resulting in becoming a social outcast. The girls who once adored him now scorn him, most of his colleagues avoid him due to the trouble he attracts, and even his partners in crime begin to scatter and leave him alone in a world of insecurities and a bleak future of squalor, hard labour and possible imprisonment.

This school pupil story portrays how you live your life is what you sow in regards to the harvest you will reap. What you do here on Earth is building your world in the afterlife/next existence as well as sculpts tomorrow. The time spent in school mirrors our life on Earth, as mankind cannot understand their purpose, so they strive for greed and power in anyway possible, inadvertently making them paupers in the spiritual/next existence.

If you are left unsure in understanding if you are walking the right path, look for signs. God/the power of good, speaks to you through others. Seek non material things as these will be granted. If you are moving in the right direction, God speaks to you directly through life's occurrences, (incidents); it is for you to be able to interpret it once you allow yourself to open your eyes, hearts and minds to eventually see it.

I see the human race strive so hard and many work their skin to the bone to achieve a state of wealth and power which gives them a level of pride, a show of self-righteousness and a stature to impress the blind around them, only to be loosing their true selves. Due to your own ignorance, self-indulgence and lack of faith/understanding, why do you try so hard to loose your soul?

In the spiritual world your time on Earth is but a blink of an eye in respect to the rest of your life, as relevant to the life of a human towards the life of a universe. PLEASE do not let mankind take away your wisdom. "THINK"!!

I was watching an academy award ceremony where the famous were so proud of themselves for what they had achieved, and all I could do is pity them, as society has blinded them all. I could see a sea of lost souls.

Parable to the above paragraph: - There is a group of people in a desert all dying of thirst; there is one container of water between them and one cup, the cup large enough to quench everyone's thirst. Yet the first one to fill their cup continues to pour, allowing the water to spill over into the sand, therefore, allowing the others to die!

Haiti tragedy

A tragedy in which close to a thousand people have died due to floods in Haiti. The floods were caused because the people of Haiti chopped down trees around their land to sell for making charcoal which made them a good living. The floods had been stopped before due to the roots of the trees absorbing the water.

There were those money-makers in high places that knew of the consequences but as usual, the world we live in puts money, power and greed before lives and destruction of what they leave behind. Exploiting the undeveloped countries by making the rabble see a fruitful life in what they sell, not understanding the outcome will destroy them. Or could it be they did know but the pleasures they could have now outweighed the tragedy which was probably not expected to affect them in their lifetime.

What irony in the above news story alone. It contains all the necessary elements for the meaning of life, of mankind, and of paradise that awaits you if only you were willing to acknowledge as a possibility.

MISFORTUNE

Questions & answers: – Why do bad things happen to me?

Believe it or not, in the spiritual world, it is only the bad things, deep emotional heartache, that allow parts of our mind (brain) to open, which could not have been open any other way. When it opens, it broadens your thoughts and makes life's problems easier to understand, 'what doesn't kill you enlightens you'.

The seed to bad things begins and ends with you; stay on the good path to eliminate falling.

Why am I ugly

Your appearance is the remnants of your previous existence and past consciousness, nether less, if you had a child who asked you the same question what would your reply be? Mankind has conditioned our minds to except beauty above all other traits. It is doubtful the way we think will be changed within our lifetime. Enhance all the other traits you have, be kind, helpful and joyful, and put the views you may have about yourself aside. This will be difficult at first but don't give in, as in time, when you meet the right partner, you will then realise what is meant by Beauty being in the eye of the beholder. You will then appreciate life for what it really is rather than mankind's twisted view.

If meeting a partner never comes to pass then remember that a spiritual life is not here for its own needs but here to help others.

If you can manage to rise above this, you can then teach others how this was accomplished, for this you shall be rewarded, if not in this life/existence but the next, have faith.

Has God given me my illness

God does not make you ill; this is the way of the world. For one to overcome the illness, one must be one with God/eternal for you to then understand it in a spiritual way. With an earth bound mind the illness will bring anguish and anger.

You are in charge of your own destiny and the predominant creator of your own outcomes. Use the ailment as a learning stage to help others overcome it if it were to happen to them. Do not let this ground you deeper into this world, use what you have to help you bloom in your next existence.

Wisdom

I do not live in your world, yet I am trapped in it and I search and fumble for a way to survive like a child taking its first steps. I question whether I will ever be able to walk on my own without the temptation of making it easier by stretching out for a helping hand, or something to grab hold off. And when I walk I will want to run, and when I run I would want to run faster than anyone else so I can be recognised and wallow in my own achievement. As a result, being blinded in not recognising those around me who could not walk!

If I could have directed those same efforts into making one other walk, would that not be more of an achievement? Even if it only be recognised by him. As it is quoted, what we do in life echoes in eternity.

As we think, so we become, inside and out, Ignorance is not bliss.

I am middle aged and have nothing to my name 'why'.

You must learn to distance yourself from earthly things and conditioning. Once you choose to acknowledge spiritual views, you will come to a realisation that you come into this world with no material goods and will leave with none.

Your purpose on earth is to help convert the bad/negative into good/positive and use your life for this purpose only; therefore you have all you need, 'YOU'. Why work your fingers to the bone for things you cannot keep? Work to build a future for your afterlife, or do you truly want to lose the major part of life by working your fingers to the bone for the purpose of reaching a false and fabricated goal, resulting in becoming a pauper in your next existence.

THE OPEN MIND and why one should believe

A man is about to go on a journey across a ten mile stretch of dessert just after having a hearty meal and drank to the full, deciding not to bring any food or water along!! Therefore, totally neglect to any unforeseen events that may occur. In the middle of the journey whilst tripping on a stone, receiving a broken ankle leaves him little hope of survival.

To keep an open mind, meaning if one believes in nothing until it is proven, leaves him with an empty cup from the start. If one believes everything until it is disproved, leaves him with a full cup until it is depleted.

Imagine a jigsaw puzzle, if you begin with too many pieces it would just be a matter of taking away those which will eventually reveal themselves as not belonging, these are simply discarded whilst remaining the finished product. (*Believing all things until disproved*).

If you leave out pieces of the puzzle it would be more difficult, as vital parts of the puzzle showing what the picture could be are not there, therefore leaving you to use your own imagination on what it may possibly be, this becomes more difficult and leaves you open to guesses. (*Not believing anything until proved*).

THE POWER OF THE MIND

We are led to believe that the mind can possibly distort matter and also communicate with other minds via telepathy. If this is true, it can metamorphose things also; therefore creating something that prior did not exist. This can also be seen as to the existence of a God or force of goodness created by the collaboration of billions of minds with the same belief, which also could explain when Christ was asked who is God, he replied, 'I am God', meaning we are all God', as without our belief he would not exist.

Or meaning if we all fight to keep our anger at bay and strive to be morally correct and righteous, then one would not need a God but is God, being as pure as one should by questioning, 'would Christ do this'?. (*We and God are all the same energy*)

There was a story in which a believed psychic answered an advert by the military who were searching for those who believed they had the gift of remote viewing. The psychic attended the gathering in a large hall full of hundreds of like-minded individuals. They were all given tests which broke the numbers down to the last few remaining psychics. One of the tests was to envisage yourself in a property at an unknown destination pointed out via a map. They were then asked to relay what they saw around them.

One particular person correctly pointed out objects around the property but it was not good enough for those in command. The remainder of those who were chosen had relayed 95% of not only the land around the property but all that was within it, including objects. Those few were then made an offer which entailed removing themselves from public life and becoming part of a secret military regiment.

Saddam Hussein once accused the US military for using their psychics to spy on him. Keep an open mind, as people of high status who have the power to access suppressed knowledge are not "crazy".

LOST MIND

I have come to learn that when you close your mind to spirituality you suppress a major part of your natural thought process, stopping you from rationalising as sensibly as you would have otherwise. This action will pyramid into making wrong choices and decisions in life. You will be adamant that what you believe and comprehend to be just, is so. Yet those who are of a spiritual nature have a far greater capacity to see beyond the wall of thought you have personally adopted.

The block you have of thinking/understanding is a process of negativity just like the build up of fat in a person's body caused by eating the wrong foods. You can not see the block it is creating for the blood to pass to your heart until catastrophe happens but a doctor can and will direct you. This is the same with a righteous spiritual person such as I; who have been blessed with a Divine sight and will direct and enlighten you.

Yet if the negativity is too dense, it is an impossible task to try and positively re-direct you, as you are on the path of your chosen destiny that nobody can change, not even you.

PSYCHIC ABILITY

This is recognised as something outside of societies understanding of normality. It currently cannot be explained or seen, therefore has no explanation whether it exists or not. In time it will be explained by the realms of science. Once technology has reached that stage of recognition and advancement all spiritual scenarios will eventually fit into scientific explanation as a fact of existence, but only if those in power decide they want mankind to know or keep us in the dark as we are at present.

When you reach a stage where you believe to have psychic or supernatural powers, you cannot help but question your own sanity. This area of thought is brought on due to society brainwashing us in believing for this to exist is insane. Yet with a few test's you can prove to yourself otherwise.

My tests

I asked a colleague to hide an object in their bedroom; my goal was to psychically find out its exact location.

My first thought was an object of jewellery. Later whilst I was about to fall asleep I had a vision of a young woman around the age of 24/28, she told me in a cheerful loud voice that my colleague had hidden it in a jewellery box, it was plain and clear as my colleague telling me directly! With no symbols or hidden messages, it was as plain as day. When I relayed the information my colleague was in awe! Not only did I relay where it was but also that the object was a ring. Whilst the woman in my vision was telling me this I was trying to ask her who she was, but to no avail. I continue with my tests, as to use the mind in this manner makes it stronger.

Another test, again, the same colleague was asked to draw a picture. My goal was to visualise what was drawn. I chose this to test how powerful mine and your abilities can be or become, taking into account the infinite amount of things that could be chosen, to then know, would be the ultimate way of proving this was real. It took me around two months to get another vision.

The process was very tiring on the mind and frustrating whilst waiting for an answer. The vision yet again was whilst I was relaxed in bed. I had prayed for help. I had a vision of a fish, when I relayed my vision to my colleague, who replied it was a dolphin they had drawn. My visions are now much stronger.

We all have this ability but due to distancing ourselves from the spiritual side of our existence we lose the greatest power mankind have.

For you to try this, do not try to think of the object drawn, you must only think of the person who drew it and visualise that person drawing and then allow a picture or vision to form.

There are dark forces in positions of power who know we have this ability but do not want mankind to know, as it will be very dangerous for them to hold onto their influence over us if we find out. So I know I will be faced with many obstacles and possible unexpected "accidents" if they suspect the world awakening to the wisdom of what I write.

SCIENCE AND SPIRITUALITY

We are in a period whereby science is trying all forms of experiments to find God. A particle acceleration experiment was carried out by scientists who are looking for questions to the beginning of the universe, and the reality is that the Atom may have the answer they are truly looking for. The Atom has shown areas of its structure that defy rationality. Science believes that parts of the Atom do not exist unless you see it/acknowledge its existence. Basically, before you see it, it does not exist.

As an example, in an episode of 'Doctor Who', there were some beings that looked like statues; they would remain that way unless you looked at them. Looking at them would give them mobility and life.

Taking the above and putting it into a certain context would suggest that we all are statues until we enlighten ourselves to a higher level of thought which will release us from the shackles we are bound to, giving us the freedom of the universe. We and the universe are all made of the same Atom, which would suggest we have its power.

Quantum electro dynamics can explain the outcome of every experiment, so science is quite happy with this level of understanding. Until the spiritual nature of the Atom is taken into perspective and we learn to use a higher level of interaction with it, we remain stagnant.

It all accumulates to a simple answer. The universe has a balance of positive and negative energies which we are all part of. The universe, mankind and all contained within it are as one. There is no distance, time or matter. Once we all come to this understanding and learn how it works and how to regulate it, we will then understand the concept of eternal existence.

Life and the atom

The atom is made of half positive and half negative energy. When atoms approach a black hole the negative half separates and is drawn into the hole causing the hole to collapse, creating a catastrophic explosion, allowing the positive remains outside the hole to emit a visible radioactive glow, allowing a warning to all.

This also explains the answer to why is evil necessary, meaning not all negative elements of life are evil as evil would not exist if '**you**' don't allow it to.

See this paragraph as the negative and positive side to each of us, as the effects in space are relevant to the effects here. All are made of atoms.

Big bang theory

Science is trying to discover when the universe or everything began. There is no beginning or end, as it does not exist.

Life's organisms/living energies have created what we believe to see, including the universes composition and all the positive and negative elements it consist of. In very simple terms, it is like when man was looking for the edge of the earth to discover there isn't one. We just keep going round and round, therefore unless mankind turns itself round to become more positive, we become the destroyers of our universe, our earth, ourselves and our offspring.

DEMONS/NEGATIVE ENERGIES

I have learnt that the more you indulge in Holy Scriptures and good deeds, the demonic energies notice by manifesting as apparitions; this is to trick and frighten you into believing it is the indulgence causing this. Do not be fooled, the source wants you to be in fear to stop your quest for enlightenment and righteousness. It cannot harm you once your faith is with 'God/peace'. Have no fear, as it is your fear that fuels the fire.

Do not jump and scream when you are at one with the other world/knowledge. Be strong and try to understand, as it is another realm in which you are in control but part of the world we live in, the world that governments and demons/negative energies do not want you to know about.

To elaborate, mixing positive and negative energies will create a disturbance we associate with "demons" ect; but it is simply both energies combining and beginning to stabilise themselves to our conscience.

HEALING

If you would like to try this gift (in which I believe we all possess but have lost through the centuries of neglect or lacking belief in its abilities), the simplest way I can explain it is to imagine your body as a Hoover, your hand as the nozzle. Whilst laying your hand on the area or above it, visualise your hand drawing out the ailment, then take your hand away from the person and reverse the process into the open space as if you are emptying the Hoover back through the nozzle and repeat. This may work immediately or may take a few sessions, endeavour. But for it to work at all, you must have full belief in what you do. Without belief this will not work, you are your own restraint.

There are two forms of healing; there is the healing of faith, consisting in the belief of God/peace and ones divinity which will heal all. And there is the healing from the body, which can only heal on a physical plain.

Take heed if you decide to go to a healing centre, as the ailment you have is there for the purpose of balancing your positive and negative elements collated in life. If you decide to live as usual without any change, removing/healing the existing ailment will just displace the negative energy to manifest in a different part of your life.

The only way it can be successful is for you to change your life to becoming righteous, and for every action you take to be for the good of everything and not merely for yourself.

The healing will then eliminate or slowly transform the ailment towards a positive path.

If it is a physical ailment it does not mean it will come back as one. It could come back as anything connected to the same emotional level.

FAIRIES, GOBLINS AND GNOMES

A woman I know told me this tale: - At the age of five whilst eating, these little people would appear and be quite annoying, as they would snatch the spoon from her and eat her food. She would say, if you see them try to grab their hat, because if you can they are vowed to offer you a wish. Family members have had encounters with these beings; they have been known to jump on their beds and pull at their feet while they were trying to sleep. A family member was in bed one night when they felt a heavy weight on their chest. Lying face up they moved their hand towards the weight and could feel the shape of a small figure. They managed to push it away but saw nothing when the room was lit.

ANGELS

Lying in bed one evening reading the Bible, my page marker being a picture of the Archangel Michael; before going to sleep I read the prayer on the back of it. That night I felt a stroking touch on my left cheek and neck. This touch was followed by the sound of bells which automatically associated the event as an angel experience. This happened twice that evening in succession. Angels are the concentrated benevolent energies of past teachers of righteousness.

SOME EXPERIENCES

Due to my enlightened insight into the spiritual world via channelling, I have been made aware of the blanket society has thrown over the population to believe and exist in a matrix world, in which will condemn oneself to a dark and unknown afterlife. This is well understood by Earths powers that be, therefore making our world controlled by evil/negative elements.

I know of a population of spiritual beings also known as star children, with the hope of bringing spirituality and morality back into our world. The idea of bringing an army of these beings rather than just the one is a tactful move. I am part of the battle to bring peace back, 'world peace from within'.

In this world there is a thin line between sanity and insanity. One must always question and test their understanding and belief of their actions and the knowledge they gain. These are some test I believed I had to do to prove my own sanity, if only to myself.

I asked a person to draw a shape, and then in it name a colour and a number. I chose all correctly, not only once but three times out of three.

Also another was asked to shuffle a full deck of English cards, he gave them back to me, I proceeded to relay the first eight cards correctly. At that point I gave them back as it was quite frightening. I could psychically see the cards on the reverse via picture form.

I have healed many a person, and have more than proved to myself with many more tests that all I write is not fantasy; '**believe**' it is real.

GHOSTS

In your lifetime, how you live your life leaves behind a ripple, just like the ripple of a pebble plunging into water. This energy which is left behind becomes and is known as your spirit. The energy can be defined as good or bad, depending on the way of life you chose to live. The reminiscence of this will add to the positive and negative elements to the growth of our existing world.

This is not you who are left behind wondering the Earth, as our souls pass on and totally move away from earthly things and family. As stated before, this is your Earth family, and in most cases, not connected to you beyond this point.

As an example: – If our whole universe explodes, our energies remain in that place; in trillions of years another universe may appear in close proximity and also be affected by the energies we leave behind. The "ghost" energy that is left behind can be contacted and occasionally manifest into a materialistic force, meaning a solid energy which can move and effect things in our own material world.

There are mediums who truly believe they are contacting your departed from the spirit world, the proof lies in what they say. Be aware that the meaning behind energy is the echo of the person who has died. Everything the dead person knew till the day of death the psychic will pick up on. Also the psychic will pick up everything the family member or friend knows and feels. All the psychic is doing is tuning into their frequency simply by being gifted with rear genetics known as a sensitive.

Proof tests

If the relative of a deceased asks a friend to hide something in a specific place without relaying it to them, and then the relative who attends the show asks the spirit to tell them where the friend has hidden it, this will be proof, as the person in the audience does not know and neither would the deceased. If you

then use this process of elimination you will find there is no medium that can do this, therefore proving my theory.
The truth is out there, it is just making sense of "A truth".

Remember, time and space has no relevance in the spirit world, therefore the spirit remains in the time of their souls departure.

Questions & answers

Do animals have souls?

Animals do not have the full intelligence of understanding right from wrong, therefore not having the free will to contribute to the spiritual element which makes up the universal balance of positive and negative. Yet their energies will remain as spirits on an earthly plain which can enhance either element.

Due to this, animals cannot be used as a firewood base to fuel either element, meaning it is not classed as a soul. Yet just as important to the balance of life.

Will I see my pet in the afterlife?

You hold the answer to its probability, as it is due to the way you live this existence that sculpts the outcome to your possible next.

Spiritual Orbs

These are pockets of energy known as our spirit, those who have contact with these have the ability to channel these forces for knowledge of the energies life and also access the time from which it came.

Requesting can allow an object from its time to manifest. You can also use its energy as a force to interact with us, resulting in moving objects, make sounds and even vocal contact. It may even be a possibility to enter the orb as a vessel for travel.

Do not confuse these as the souls of the departed; they are the energies the once living left behind as previously explained.

TIME TRAVEL

It is possible for one to travel in time. You can also change a past event, but this will not change our future. It will create an alternate future/dimension. These alternate dimensions will run side by side with ours. If you went back and killed yourself you would not erase your existing future self.

If you travel into the future, it would be impossible to calculate which future you enter, as each decision you make creates an alternate future, therefore there are innumerable futures. This would suggest that you cannot change your life by tampering with time. Think carefully on the decision you make today as this is final. The only important thing you need to know is how to make the right decision; you make that first step by acknowledging this book.

There is no possible action you can conceive that does not already exist, or taken place, as you're past and future has already happened and run simultaneously. It is your present actions that define were you are placed within that time frame.

There are moments in time where time holes can open. These are natural metrological disturbances, (commonly known as white holes), that are as natural as a twister. In time, (if science does not already know and suppressed it from us), science will learn to understand how they work, including when and where they will open. These time holes are on Earth and in space. If you enter one that is back in time, you will be able to see the past differences, but those from the past will not see yours, as anything you have which did not exist in the past reverts to their time. As an example a car may revert to a horse and cart.

Tampering with time can create a paradox effect, as to change an event will create a life force on another dimensional sphere who's energy will interact and effect our world.

GLIMPSE INTO THE FUTURE

The existence of an afterlife will be proved by a simple mathematical equation which will in turn be the beginning of true education.

Telepathy will be taught as part of normal education but will have a necessity to be controlled by law and the adjustment of the elements which contains the means of preventing its function. Psychics will also be acknowledged as normal and will be used to contact passed energies to solve crime and many other areas, as passed time is always visible.

Holes in matter will be detected. The openings will be found just like radar detecting aircraft. These will eventually be controlled, created and used as a form of teleportation/travel. Long distances will be like walking through a door into the next room.

Mankind's negative DNA can be manipulated at birth, enabling the individual to be incapable of criminal thought. This should not be allowed as it will take away free will which is the soul; this process will allow those who still have it, to reign over the population and turn mankind into a robotic state; this will then be the end of all creation. Negativity is a necessary element required for the continuation of all creativity. It is to be controlled by educating mankind to the true purpose of life and our afterlife.

RELIGION

Unexplained phenomena may have attributed to ancient man's belief in a God, whether it being natural, extraterrestrial, man's creation of time travel, heavenly and spiritual amongst many other probabilities. Fear of the unknown, of a power beyond our knowledge and control can be interpreted as God.

Mankind's weakness in understanding what they see reduced them to, (what proof do we have for the existence of a heavenly body). As an example: Visions of Christ are seen by mankind as what we are led to believe he looks like, also of his mother the Virgin Mary and many other's!! One of many other reasons why we believe he looks like this is due to a shroud, (the Turin shroud), believed to have been placed on his body, leaving his impression. He also appeared to a nun who painted him, and many other scenarios. Are these real apparitions or just a state of mind?

The shroud and also a cloth believed to have been used to wipe the face of Christ as he fell, both had the same DNA!

Further examples include the Bible, the Dead Sea Scrolls, the Bible Codes! Life after death scenarios, reincarnation, the greatest evidence for me, 'aside from what I now know', is the birth of Christ recorded in history, other than the gospels, (the Star of David), (the three wise kings). History denotes that higher powers on earth knew of the Childs birth somehow. Due to these reasons King Herod ordered the execution of every fist born, and a king's intervention was not just towards Christ but also Moses and John the Baptist. This goes to show that those in power have more knowledge of so called "heavenly interventions and alchemy" then we are led to believe or would ever believe possible.

So basically this tells us a special being was here but still does not prove where he was from. Was it a heavenly body or a higher intelligence that was trying to help the human race? As time goes on it seems to be backfiring, as now it is a battle to who's God or faith is the real or the stronger. Basically what has happened is humanities Neanderthal mentality has been brought into the equation, therefore throwing a spanner in the works.

To stick to one religion is like one branch of a police force taking the responsibility to find an assailant, when they could find the assailant much quicker if they shared the knowledge with all branches and worked together. For their own selfish reasons and personal acknowledgment they lose the sense of true purpose and justice. Religion should be seen as a base to where you begin to learn right from wrong, be it the reason why humanity needs or needed a God. From there you would have built a foundation strong enough for you to use your own common sense to differentiate fact from fiction.

Religious symbols should not be made welcome in schools. A school should be acknowledged as a learning place for all who attend to be made aware of a one/singular being; a respect of peace to your fellow human being and not to force your religion or any other form of segregation onto others by the means of religious objects being worn. One should enter a school with that respect and that moral understanding. Those who chose not to be as one should not be welcome. If you cannot reform and show a value of being one with all, for the sake of peace and understanding, you must then question your true value.

Religion should be seen as a personal part of ones life. We can all see and acknowledge different faiths and beliefs which lead to peace and have free will to follow whomever we wish to, and it should be left to each individual to do so. But once chosen should not be 'forced' upon another.

One must have the belief in a higher presence to make sense of life, or life would be meaningless. One arrives to a level of intelligence and wisdom to pass onto their offspring. For example, if the world was to explode tomorrow, what would the purpose of anything earthly be?

If there was no spiritual guidance to follow, then morality, justice and all that has a purpose would not exist, and the human race would tumble into destruction against his fellow man and evil would rein. Therefore, man would be creating a living hell for their offspring, and if there is reincarnation, then all you are doing is destroying yourself. Be wise, as you do not really know the truth. If you were to make a bet on a 50/50 chance, would you really stake everything you own? If you were given a million pound bet to answer a question correctly on a certain subject, would you not study that subject first before giving your answer?

The evidence must be acknowledged before a person is judged.

The greatest of all, is that individual who has no need of religious beliefs and yet does good deeds and follows the path of righteousness.

Questions & answers –

Why is the greatest person, one who has no religious beliefs yet is righteous?

Because it is not anything they have to fear that guides them, be it a being/creator or the outcome of an afterlife, and neither a belief in karma to divert them. Yet have the simple understanding and nature, allowing them the wisdom to justify the act of doing good is how life should 'BE'.

One must understand the implications of what righteous means, and how to live a righteous life, or what one needs to do to be recognised as being righteous; allow the beatitudes to be your guide and what is hereby written.

THE CHURCH TODAY

Jesus says we are here to serve not to be served; this quotation shows the hypocrisy in our existing religions! The Roman church wants the world to follow their beliefs and faiths, yet if their followers do not go to church every week they do not allow them to marry, be christened, or allow their children to go to catholic schools, therefore pushing them away from that which they are trying to attract them to in the first place. And how can anyone follow the hypocrisy of having a pope who resides in a palace of gold in which value in itself can save the lives of millions; yet its money is put towards idols and trinkets. A true faith would remove these spiritually worthless trinket's and use them to generate an income towards saving those in true need, and teaching others of the sin in having riches, as is stated in this book elsewhere.

The church has taken the same views as Lazarus prior to being brought back to life. This applies to all religions. Lazarus being the best friend of Jesus who explained of how his wealth helps the many, to which Jesus replied 'it is easier for a camel to pass through the eye of a needle then for a rich man to enter the gates of Heaven'!

We may spend billions on goods for ourselves and the family. For example: - mansions, fast cars, gold, designer wear. All these can become an investment to make more money for you in the future, but when you die you take nothing of this with you. Spiritually what you take to your next existence is a suitcase of 'sorrow' and a suitcase of 'love'. With that money, many lives could have been enhanced. Many tears could have been averted. Many children could have been saved from abuse and starvation.

In heaven you hear the echo of the lives you have changed as you enter its gates. The materialist properties bought on Earth by man-made money are to be left to those who deserve it. Only your 'soul/conscience' passes on after death.

Do not let society's selfishness; greed and personal vanity take away your greatest reward that awaits you, which you can help build for yourself whilst in life.

Priests ask to be called father, when most are not worthy, as they are all blind and follow a religious lie gladly. Those who are worthy should be named Shepherd's, as there is only one father and that is the Holy Father, the creator, (consciousness).

If a church was just an empty shell and the priest earned just enough to get buy, and gave respect to those who live their lives by treating thy fellow man as they would be treated, and teach those same principles to their children and use the Bible as a guide. Would that not be a worthier way in which to follow, now and for the future of all mankind?

No form of clothing, pendants or jewellery etc, should be necessary to enter a holy place. To stop any person entering due to their attire is a sin. As long as the person is not entering to purposely offend, e.g. to walk into a holy place fully naked whilst others are there can be offensive. One can be offered a blanket to cover the waist area and should be made welcome.

Your faith is on the inside not the outside.

Questions and answers –

Is it necessary to go to church?

Spiritually it is not necessary for obtaining the love of the father, (attracting positive energies). But it would be nice to visit occasionally.

It would be like leaving home, although you love your parents and keep in touch, it is not the same as occasionally visiting them. Although the faith that built the church has lost its way, the building itself is a holy place.

Do I need to pray?

This has a connection to the above question; your home expects you to keep in touch. To pray also enhances the spiritual senses. When one prays it accesses positive energies and if done with emotional feeling/content is a form of meditation.

I want to become a priest but I don't agree with church processes, what do you advise

If you want to lead your life the way of the father/good deeds, then use your life for others. This can be learned by the life of Maria Teresa, discarding the belief in physical suffering. (As the prophet's teachings of suffering is to avoid the cultural misconception of material success), not physical pain. Go into the world and convert wrong doers to do good deeds. The priesthood is a man made religion not the teachings of Jesus and the prophets.

Should I become a nun?

This applies to the previous question. If your faith is strong, you are here to serve and not be served. Your life hence should be for the benefit of the needy. To become a nun may hold you back and allow humanities bureaucracy to cloud your true purpose.

BUDDHISM

Many would question, if all creatures are sacred then why would God create the wilds of the jungle where one cannot live without the devouring of another? If this was so and all creatures are to be sacred, then why did God make them carnivores instead of vegetarians who would live off the land and therefore so should follow man, yet it is not so.

To understand this paragraph, God did not create the Earth; God created intelligence. Evolution was the way of the land until that point, e.g. the evolution of a combined consciousness.

But take heed. This does not give you the right to abuse animals; you must at all times respect life no mater how small. If something can be saved, then this is the path you must take.

Although the larger species are recognised as food, if there is an alternative, 'we', as "civilised" beings must follow this path. But also be aware that the Earths powers that be can utilise this process to create a deficiency in humanity for their personal "greater" selfish purpose. One must scrutinise and test all foods. (The Earths "powers that be" are the silent ones who truly run our planet); a secret society of unscrupulous beings that guide us like sheep to the slaughter.

When you squat a fly, question what gives you the right to judge life or death, when you can simply capture and release it back into the wild. The fly does not know of any harm it may unwittingly do, therefore is not guilty of any crime or wrong doing. If you can then judge a life, what gives you the right to condemn those who then wrongly judge you?

Meditation

In some religions you are told that meditation and chanting is required for you to reach a heavenly/enlightened state of mind. The act of meditation is not a necessity. You do not need to perform a physical action for you to achieve this. All you need to have is faith and a strong belief in yourself. You must lead a righteous lifestyle and treat all as you expect to be treated. As a guide, follow the Beatitudes of Christ and positive spiritual world teachings. This positive attitude will then open areas of your mind that you would never think possible. You then, can and will become a very spiritually powerful person. Doing this correctly will give you eternal life and powers beyond belief. This will include psychic and healing powers as an example of some of its smaller attributes. The larger picture is that it will give you a direct connection to the heavenly father/creator.

Yet for many the act of meditation helps in the aid of reaching that mind set, if required, this should then be done with the 'admiration' of its teacher and not the worship of them.

THE OLD TESTAMENT

What you must try to comprehend is that God/essence of God is complete good. It is impossible for this force to be negative in any way. This would confirm that stories of death and destruction acted in the name of God were not of God, there was a higher intelligence at work, alien to mankind. This is why the Ark of the Covenant was constructed to interact with 'that' God. God can not, and does not require objects to be contacted. For example, why would it be necessary for you to require a vessel to contact yourself, the mere suggestion is ludicrous.

The only rationalisation for this action from an alien race can only have been to gain some form of control over mankind, by using their advanced technology to sculpt a society in believe in a false God, for the purpose of a future plan.

These beings are one or a sum of many alien races which exist outside of our knowledge, and suppressed by our government. Christ was mainly a creation manifested by the benevolent ones. These are a race of beings whose world has conformed to the scientific truth of a God. They have come to realise the reality and existence of a God like energy which is part of the universes natural composition. Christ's composition and teachings are the way to eternal life/eternal light.

Much of the Old Testament was built up by an unknown race consisting of a higher intelligence around a religious reform. Therefore it was like our churches today, who teach their beliefs and not that of their prophets for their own purposes.

For any prophet from the past to have done negative things, would mean they were not prophets of God, they were led to believe so and gave all for the belief of "their" God.

A wise and just man should question any action that promotes a wrong doing, even if you believe it is from God. If it is a wrongdoing then you have been deceived.

The God our and connected benevolence create is forgiving, but the negativity created in the belief of a perceived God is still a sin. Therefore the chemical and scientific build up of our existing world cannot forgive/erase negative actions; suggesting past and present prophets who are connected to wrong deeds will do penance for that discretion in the same way as breaking the laws of our commandments and with the same punishment of all sinners.

If the above is confusing, try to understand that each being is not one but many. Due to the thoughts of who we are in the minds of those we influence, each will take a portrayal of you into their afterlife. The collaboration of these thoughts will entwine with yours, creating what your possible next existence may become!

Many of you who ridicule the belief in other worldly life outside ours, or of higher intelligence of some kind, will look upon these things as completely outrageous foolery, and there is nothing I could say that could convince you otherwise. Yet heed my words. It is very possible that in our lifetime some form of contact will be confirmed. Do not allow the shock of this to denounce the existence of a God. Learn by what is written within this book and embrace God's existence. *There is truth beyond knowledge, only the fool denies it.*

UFO

Many doubt the existence of beings outside of our own, yet without experiencing it personally; I also may have questioned the validity. I have now come to believe these beings to be a benevolent race that are in some form of contact with me. Many have tried to contact these beings in the same way as I but have not been as successful. I have come to learn that this is due to a lack of benevolence, whether it be in the faith of the Lord Jesus and Holy Spirit, or towards a higher spiritual guidance, therefore lacking the benevolence required allowing the psychic connection to take place. I used Jesus and Holy Spirit, as through my quest to seek these beings I found this to be a significant key factor!

If this is not your belief then all that is required is your faith in a higher spiritual presence and that you lead a just life. This is a necessity or all your endeavours will be in vain. Read the wisdom given by this Holy man, as it will guide you to life's hidden secrets and knowledge. The Beatitudes can be the seeds to your growth.

I have come to learn that these beings can be contacted by anyone, but mostly by those who have a pure heart and preferably no fear.

You will find that spectacular or different events are used as a cover for UFO activity. When you here of these events it is wise for ufologists to keep an open eye and mind. I have been in contact with these beings since my teenage years. They are now a guide to me which I am truly grateful.

If aliens exist does this mean there isn't a God?

Extra terrestrials are an extension of our own world, only the ignorant dismiss this. Where there is intelligence there also is a soul and therefore lays God/positive energy.

Was Christ an Alien?

No, he was a manifestation of God/positive energy, cultivated by a benevolent race/existence. What we should recognise as truly being the son of God, cultivated by good seed.

GOD

Thou shall **NOT** fear God, only as one should fear a loving father. A loving father will be angry at you if you go against his will 'because' he cares for your safety; he loves you and does not want you to get hurt. Never fear God as you would a slave master, for this can be seen as an insult to the creator, therefore portrayed as a sin. The way to be is to love God with all your heart and soul, for God, (the energy), then would put no other before you.

As an example of the connection between humanity and God. God is the car, you hold the key to open the car and put it in motion, and you are also in control of how you drive it. The car can keep you out of the rain and cold, give you a comfortable and enjoyable journey, entertain you with music of your choice; it can lighten your load and add many other benefits to your life. Yet if you neglect it, it will break down. If you drive it with no due respect, it will bring harm and danger, not only to you but also to others. You can now see the association with you and God, do good and you will reap the rewards, do harm and reap the harvest of your wrongdoings.

If God is the creator of man and the universe, the all seeing into the past, present and future, then why did he allow mankind to exist knowing of the Roman Empire and war atrocities? This would suggest that God did not know the outcome of "his" apparent creation and does not know the future, therefore suggesting there is no destiny but that which you create yourself! To try and reason and understand the creation of God as 'we' perceive it is a pointless action.

The only justification for a God is to try and understand what it tries to portray and teach us what is good and bad, and to separate good/positive from evil/negative.

Did God create the earth?

Not as we have been led to understand it. The Earth was a part of evolution, the evolution of conscience. Evolution, science and God are all connected. God is all good, (positive energy); he/she, the force would not and could not create a world in which one would need to devour another to exist. Although humanity was a benevolent creation, our actions are of freewill, for the purpose of empowering us with the key to our own heaven or hell, destiny is in our hands.

If there was a parliamentary vote and the only count that

separates them is one, it is your vote that will decide who wins. This is why in life you are the most important person, as it is your choice and vote which will decide if we fall into degradation or rise from the ashes of a broken world.

We know that earth was not the first planet created!! The energies that existed before its creation which we associate with God is what made the earth, but only in an evolutionary manner. It took the awakening of mans free will to manifest the spiritual energy which we now commonly recognise as God.

Why did God create us?

One must first understand what God is. God as humanity have named is the first energy force to obtain a conscience of ones self, basically an acknowledgement of its own existence. Its core existence is built up of positive and negative elements/energy; therefore we are an evolutionary product of Gods conscience for the purpose of adding towards the balance of those core elements.

To expand further, it is like the evolution of an animal in the wild whose physical changes have been necessary for its own future survival. The difference is understanding evolution in a spiritual nature. Basically we were created for Gods survival, for the continuation of that energy source, and it was hence from our combined consciences that 'our' God was created.

Questions & answers –

If we created God then why is he in charge?

To explain this I must go back to the seed theory. If you plant a seed for the tree to then grow, we cannot control how the trees will form or which way the roots sprout. The tree takes its own direction; all we can do is mind it/ take care of it.

You see we grew the tree to feed us, like owning a farm and planting a crop for your own survival. If we do the write thing by it, it will feed us and keep us alive. If we neglect it, it will wither, sprout bad fruit and eventually die.

Why does God tell us in the Old Testament that he created the world when you say otherwise?

The answer is one of the same; conscience/God was the beginning and creator of everything. It then took the combination of further consciences such as us to culminate in the evolution of our God and an individually recognised world. Mankind was less wise to understand science back then, and at present continues to be. Do not get bogged down by the politics/red tape of past direction/guidance, as it is the principle and wisdom to which the statements lead to which you should focus on. View the preaching's of Jesus, as he is the evolution of our creators' teachings. Also read my paragraph regarding the Old Testament. Every single person is the creator of their own world and relevant lifetimes which is created by their actions.

WHO WAS JESUS

Before I start this section I would like to spread some words of wisdom, in the words of Jesus: -

Those that are mine will know me, and if they follow me I will know them.

I have come to believe that Jesus was truly the Son of God, but also in the sense that we all can be. (I use the word God as society's commonly known expression of interpreting a higher existence).

I have been led to envisage God as a force, a collective power of goodness. I have come to understand that we leave this world with nothing. The only thing that counts and is of any value is those whose conduct and beliefs in the morality of life we change to understand and separate good from evil, to be able to define good and evil and to be able to take control over our genetic inherited evil. (To master the capability of controlling ones emotions).

We must educate ourselves to understand that in the spiritual world our status, wealth, and respect is built whist on Earth, and that our family on Earth, being each member, is a single soul, a separate entity. Meaning your current family are simply obstacles containing good or evil. On a spiritual level we are all separate entities. Christ once said 'No prophet is recognised in his own home', this is due to the above, for example, when your brother is seen as a prophet, wise and holy by others, to you he is still your brother because you lack the sight to see his soul as a spiritual manifestation beyond earthly values.

We can all have the divinity to create miracles if one's mind can be tuned into understanding this. To try and comprehend that if one kills a member of your family and then to reap revenge would only be harming oneself. To protect yourself and others is not a sin, but to needlessly kill in doing so IS!! (Protect in a non-violent manner).

Questioning ones morality: -

Then I ask myself this question! If you were armed and from a distance another armed man walks up to your brother from behind, raises his gun to the back of his head with the aim to kill him. If you had the capability to shoot dead the assailant and save your brother, 'would it be a sin'? As Christ said in his beatitudes: - Blessed are the pure in heart for they shall see God! And 'yes', in the commandments it says though shalt not KILL. Would Jesus have slain a roman to save an apostle? By my understanding I would say no, as when one of the apostles was struck on the left hand side of his face, Jesus said unto him, 'if he strikes you then turn your head and offer him your right hand side also'. Also, Peter attacking and slicing off the ear of a roman soldier sent to arrest Jesus in the aim of protecting him, Jesus swiftly told him to put away his sword, as he who lives by the sword dies by the sword. Did the saints try to build a rebellion to save him, 'no', as Jesus would have condemned this.

As previously stated, 'to save the life of your brother', if one takes all measures to stop the assailant in a just way, not to directly kill, in this case if the assailant died by your hand it would not be a direct sin but one nevertheless. This would be seen as protecting a life by the wisdom of God. Thereafter, Gods will, will be done, as the negativity caused by death cannot be eradicated and penance would be due.

Try to understand that if you follow a righteous life your creator/positive energies would never allow you to fall into such a situation, regarding the brother situation stated.
Therefore you will never have to question your actions; the devil/negative energies will be repelled. Preventing the action rather than searching for the cure.

This suggests, seeing God one must truly believe they are pure in heart, but to truly be the Son of God, one must follow the commandments laid down by our spiritual creator. Once you can understand and follow these beliefs even in the beginning stages, you "WILL" feel a presence of holiness, an overwhelming power of serenity and of someone guiding you, and God will grant you certain wishes.

Do not ask directly, e.g. If your looking for a job due to being unemployed, ask for the strength and wisdom to do so, as without helping yourself the whole process of your request will be meaningless. 'To truly ask and believe, accesses elements outside of our understanding and allows positive energies to guide and balance our negative fields'.

People today still ask of who killed Jesus. It is irrelevant. It does not matter how much you would like to lay the blame, as Christ has already forgiven those who were accountable from the cross. For you to then condemn them is to question Christ himself. Change the world by changing yourself, by removing negativity from within.

I would like to say in respect to what I have written, at this moment in time I have nothing to show for my life except the love of a good family and a group of friends I can truly trust. Materialistically I entered this world with nothing and will leave with nothing, but spiritually I leave behind warm hearts, loving memories and the hope/seed of a new and peaceful life for many, as the legacy of what I leave behind makes the phrase, 'the best things in life are free', a true reality.

When Jesus said, 'no one passes into the gates of heaven but through me', means himself being you, as you and only you hold the key. As it is your free will which guides you, and your decision which makes you pure, good or evil.

Always remember to follow the laws and wisdom of Jesus and those prophets who condone any form of death and destruction. Jesus brought the evolution of faith from his and our creator. You, as I, once enlightened, continue to evolve as the crop from the seed of Christ.

If you wrong your creator and ponder on what the creators emotions to this would be, then picture yourself as the parent to your rebellious child.

There are many who question what race Jesus was from, also the time and place in which Jesus existed. You must comprehend that history has been tampered with to suit the masses. Do not let all this subterfuge distance you from the **moral** teachings of such a man and those of many prophets. Allow these teachings to give birth to your wisdom. Once you begin to follow the beatitudes and lead such an existence, all your questions will be answered. Once you reach that stage, you would have found him to a point where you will have no further questions but will be he who gives the answers.

If still in doubt that the story of Christ's existence be a possible myth, then the person who created the myth would be the equivalent of the Christ, as he is the teacher of righteousness, as through the persons story many have been converted to do good, to which justifies the persons aim! You must seek the purpose and final outcome rather than question its validity, for there lays God.

If one still truly feels the need of expert proof to the existence of Christ, then, declared to be the greatest of experts that the world had ever known, Professor of law at Harvard 'Simon Greenleaf' who was Jewish and a non believer of Christ, decided to make an investigation into the validity of Christ and finally concluded that any unbiased jury in the world would have to conclude that Jesus and his history are all true and it is for the non believer to prove otherwise. He has written a book on his findings called – The Testimony of The Evangelists.

Questions & answers

In this book it says the world is our own creation. If the world 'is' our own creation and we are here of sin and hence the world being of sin, then how come Jesus was here?

Jesus is the energy of mankind's misunderstanding of righteousness/benevolence, therefore he also is here from our sin, to which he battled, used and converted to righteousness, having to suffer the pain and sacrifice of converting the sin 'within' to good.

Was Jesus a virgin birth: -

Many religions would like you to believe this so they may have full reign over Jesus, for the purpose in hiding the fact that we all can become as Jesus.

Jesus was truly born when St John the Baptist baptised him, therefore recognised as a virgin birth, (being born again by his creator and not of flesh). *Romans 1:3. Christ our lord which was made of the seed of David according to the flesh.*

Do not let this demean him, as this should enlighten you in recognising Jesus as flesh and blood, with feelings, emotions and weaknesses just as you and I, therefore should be recognised as greater than we could ever possibly conceive.

With the barrier removed from being born of a God in the physical sense, we should no longer use this excuse for our own deviation of righteousness. If he as one person can follow this road to a peaceful existence, we can do this also, imagine how our lives would be if we all follow his ways.

His miracles, his love and his peace can be yours and mine!

He gave his life to 'truly' save yours.

Matthew 10:34

Do not think that I come to bring peace on earth; I did not come to bring peace but a sword. For I have come to set a man against his father, a daughter against her mother and a daughter-in-law against her mother-in-law; and a man's enemies will be those of his own household.

He who loves father or mother more than me is not worthy of me, and he who loves son or daughter more than me is not worthy of me, and he who does not take his cross and follow after me is not worthy of me. He who finds his life will lose it and he who loses his life for my sake will find it.

Matthews verse explained

Do not think that I come to bring peace on earth;

Since you now have conscience, the earth is your creation and not mine, therefore how can I bring peace when you have chosen otherwise.

I did not come to bring peace but a sword. For I have come to set a man against his father, a daughter against her mother and a daughter-in-law against her mother-in-law;

Due to the earth not being a peaceful creation would mean you have created it from a negative passed existence sculpted by the sword, 'your sword', signifying the wrongs you done. If it wasn't so, you wouldn't be here.

Just as the Christians were slaughtered for their beliefs, so must you, as evil cannot be defeated in battle because battle is a negative. Total faith means your belief in the afterlife, not this one. Their deaths gave life to thousands of positive elements/energies for the power and existence of God, therefore being defeat in death.

And a man's enemies will be those of his own household.

This verse shows the psychology of mankind. As an example: - if a member of your family strives for fame, in the process of this, the member is scolded and mocked, as such - ('don't live in a fairytale, do a normal job fool'.) But when the member makes it, all that have mocked are the first to associate themselves to this now 'favoured' individual, jealous hypocrite's. Fame was used as an example; fame has no worth if righteous.

He who loves father or mother more than me is not worthy of me, and he who loves son or daughter more than me is not worthy of me.

You are the children of one creator/consciousness. You are a single and separate soul; all others are just pawns for your interaction and enlightenment. Do not allow these other entities to stop you seeking righteousness.

He who does not take his cross and follow after me is not worthy of me. He who finds his life will lose it and he who loses his life for my sake will find it.

You are here to serve and not be served. There is no room for vanity or such as the selfishness of humanities craving for "self respect"; fame, nobility, possessions, pride, power and success are the traps of society. Your life should have one purpose and that is to convert all to peace. To your understanding, leaving the previous mentioned behind, is taking up his/your cross. Do not strive for those cravings, as it then takes away your true purpose and the grace of your following existence.

FAITH

Sometimes following a faith can feel harrowing. It can overcome you and make you rebel, as you associate it as an angry parent or strict school teacher, even a resentful boss who has it in for you. Fight these feelings, as these negative feelings will be the breaking of you. There should be no God or faith which is forcing its wisdom upon you.

The reason why it is there is to allow you to understand the way of the world. As an example, parents know that a certain action their child is about to take will end in the child's harm. The child will take offence in you telling them what to do and take a disliking to you, yet as you are of greater wisdom who knows of the dangers; you are only protecting the child and informing them of an outcome. This is the same as God/natures elements do to you. Try to visualise it as a loving parent who cares for you deeply, do not push love away. Embrace it.

SAINT JUDAS

Those who truly believe in Christ our saviour should try to comprehend what it would have been like walking with him as one of his apostles, witnessing many of his miracles, hearing his wisdom. To be in such a person's presence for three years and then betray him would be ludicrous. Christ new of his demise, as this was not only predicted in the Old Testament but also predicted by him. This action was necessary for him to achieve his goal. The whole purpose of his being was tied into this moment of death and resurrection, therefore it must be done. He would have needed to ask one of his apostles who would be strong enough to pretend to betray him and know that the apostles' name could be branded a traitor, possibly for eternity.

Judas was that apostle who volunteered. For this man to comprehend his fate for future generations was a great and noble deed. He did not commit suicide, as this would go against all Christ had taught him; he was killed by the same people who condemned Christ for the purpose of making history believe Christ could be betrayed, to make us believe that Christ was just a man and not our saviour. BELIEVE what I say, as to believe, 'they' would have failed and the blessed name of Saint Judas can finally be vindicated as being one of the greatest of his followers.

THE DA VINCI CODES

Did Jesus have children? This is a very simple question for the divine. Jesus was divine to such a strength that only one who can understand his divinity can understand that he would never bare the responsibility of adding another soul to a damned world. The Da Vinci secret has been confused by covering a lie by the Church of an existing lie.

One possible truth being to conceal the fact that woman were as important to his teaching as to what man is, if not even more so. There is no discrimination in faith except for the faithless.

PARABLES

The reason why Christ spoke in parables is quite straightforward. If you say something directly to a hundred people which is of a specific significance, each person will interpret it in different ways. A certain scenario can only be explained to select people in different ways, therefore a necessity to convert to a parable being in its own way a virtual story.

A person can listen to a story but due to the way they perceive and understand life and its surroundings will interpret the story to their own version of its meaning.

A righteous man will see a totally different outcome to those who live their life on the opposite side of the moral spectrum, therefore distinguishing those who deserve to be told the story from those who are beyond the help they choose to push aside.

A parable is a necessity for the reason that one cannot tell another what to do, as a command taken out of context can result in negative energies befalling the advisor. You must never directly tell another what to do. For you to give safe positive advice you must relay it either in a philosophical saying, a parable or as a story relating to the question.

The Parable connecting driving a car and life

Life can be like driving a car. If you get into your car and start the journey in haste, a state of urgency, then you must try to calm yourself beforehand. Master your own emotions or you will lose them into the control of evil/negativity. If you recognise all other drivers on the road as being yourself this will be a beginning.

When you see someone speed past you, do you not look at them in disgust, then why shouldn't others see you in the same manner when you do it? Due to your personal selfishness and joyful indulgence in speed you not only risk you and your passenger's life but also innocent bystanders. You are literally playing with their lives like Russian roulette. If a speeding driver is responsible for the death of a family member, due to any reason, like speed, alcohol, messing around causing them to take their eyes off the road, etc, then how would you feel towards this person? Then what gives you the right to do the same?

If you drive without patience and look upon other drivers as objects and neglect the above, then anger and stress will start from the beginning of your journey. You tend to believe the road is yours only, to do as you please and all others are a hindrance. The smallest mistake another driver makes will be exaggerated in your eyes and result in making the outcome 100 times worse than what it is, causing road rage, resulting in a possible confrontation, and in the worse cases imprisonment due to your outburst. FOR WHAT!! If you reason with yourself, the only cause to the whole incident was YOU.

If you follow the first paragraph by starting calmly and respecting others, then your journey will start gracefully. Patience will drive you in grace; the drive itself can become a stress reliever, listening to your favourite music and even singing along, cruising slowly and enjoying your surroundings whilst understanding the needs of other drivers and the reasons to some of their mistakes to which you must comprehend are mostly accidental. We are all human and we all make mistakes.

Be compassionate and forgiving, as the result will be like taking the action towards yourself. The reward will be yours.

This book can be recognised as a parable

This book is like a parable. Many will criticise, others will analyse but many of you will recognise aspects of themselves and will be awoken to the realisation that you are not alone and need not ask any questions, as those of you 'know', in the same respect as when one is truly in love 'YOU KNOW'.

We do not remember choosing to be here. It is like being accused and sent to prison for a crime we did not commit. First thing you would feel is fear. The wisest thing to do is to mix with the right group compromising in good deeds, who want to survive their time unscathed and as safe and easy as possible, who will give you their help, experience and guidance, uncontaminated by the negative elements surrounding them.

Repent, change your life now, fight the anger within and aim that energy to loving your neighbour, in doing this you not only help others but you are saving yourself.

We are here to serve, not to be served.

THOU SHALT NOT KILL? Questioning reason.

This is a commandment which many question. Does this mean you should not kill full stop? This would suggest you kill nothing, from an ant to a human. But if you look at it from a moral standard, knowing what I know and preaching what I preach.

If I was held against my own will with, lets say helpless children, by a person who abused us and knowing this would go on; having to stand by and watch this person abuse continually ending in our death; if there was only 'one' choice/action remaining due to all peaceful avenues failing, resulting in the possible 'accidental' death of the assailant by stopping him, I personally, in that scenario, would then take that option. Even knowing it may be condemning me in my next existence, so be it. I could not justify any faith that would expect you to standby and not take that chance whilst innocent helpless children are tortured in this manner. Therefore, I justify the Archangel Michael's destruction of evil, as to 'protect' by the use of aggravated force for 'extreme' moral purposes, and can 'to an extent' be justified in the same regards as accidentally losing your own life in an action to save another. The difference being, you can in 'some' circumstances be martyred for sacrificing your own life but there is no pride or exoneration if taking of one even when justified.

Some would question this by saying it was destined for those children to be in those circumstances, stating: - 'It is the will of God'. But how can it be the will of God when it is being done by evil? The work of the devil/negative energies that is within us all. Yet these children may have been bad in a prior existence, therefore the creators of their own demise, and for you to intervene sets you up for your own downfall and another win for the devil. I then ask the question, none of us truly know and can only rely on our faith/moral understanding. Yet within my heart and my soul and following my faith through channelling, I believe the above statement to be justified and would leave my fate in the hands of our creator and the evolution of his commandments by his righteousness Jesus Christ, as it is written; no one goes to heaven but through him!

Still I ask the question, if I was the devil and knew how strong a person's faith really was and I truly wanted his soul, I would know the temptation of the above circumstances would just about do it, "the devil laughs last"?

The only way to avoid temptation is to try and keep a distance from it. If one was born into temptation how does that person avoid the Devils web, once dumped into a vipers den and knows no different!! Could it be you who is the outside intervention that has seen the light and has the divinity to guide and shepherd them from the valley of darkness? Could you be the human equivalent of the Angel we all crave?

If there was not 100% proof of the existence of something, e.g. if someone tells you to jump from a bridge as there is an air distortion that will catch you and you will float gently to the ground; would you take their word and jump? Even though you have read books on it and have had many witnesses!! I do not think so. So then why would you kill (sin) for the apparent existence of an entity of which you have no solid proof to its existence? Another example follows. I heard the other day that a person has taped silence and is now selling it to the public. Most of the sane or half intelligent would not spend their hard earned money on something that they do not even know is there!! All you have to go on is the faith which is created by our upbringing and societies brainwashing, and I do believe that a God, whose property is peace, condones killing not promotes it.

'PLEASE THINK'. To take an innocent life is not martyrdom. To kill for your faith is the work of the Devil, (Evil), and you will be judged in the fitting way you judged those innocent people whose life you took by the God you selfishly believe only you know. Your prophet has not mislead you, humanity has.

We are living in a world to which I believe a very small percentage of the population truly believe in world peace and helping thy neighbour, and that percentage of which can rationalise between reality and scepticism. Those of you who believe in killing for a faith should step out of yourselves and see yourselves for what you really are, 'EVIL'! You have become what you are trying to eradicate, a virus to the rest of the world to which you will help to destroy. And yet the perfect candidate for government world population reduction, as they know that for the world to survive, the population has to be reduced, whether it is by disease, war or with the help of fundamentalist. War generates money for the merciless.

One is spoken to by God/positive energies through the righteous, (those who do good deeds), as one is lead by the Devil/negative energies though evil men! (Those who do wrong deeds).

For this paragraph to be read by mankind can create utter destruction, as mans fallibility and selfishness would twist it out of all proportion to justify their own purpose for their craving to kill. Be warned, to do this would be to your own destruction in this life and the next.

For your quest of enlightenment you must avoid killing any form of life. In the society we live in, to not kill may not make sense to many but that is because the world has lost its way and this is why we come across many stumbling blocks and difficult questions. Due to mankind's own inequities, to kill has become part of its existence which can be erased if it was not for humanities selfishness and greed. As stated before, once you become righteous you will be protected by forces above any protection the world can give, resulting in these situations never to be put before you.

Honour killing

A father believes his daughter is seeing another man against the family's wishes and 'suspects' she may have slept with him, then takes it upon himself to kill her.

Many in this world live in a delusional belief that has been etched into their minds since birth by the ignorance of their surroundings. This goes to show the lack of stability in the mind of the human race. For a parent to believe, 'without a doubt', that the honourable thing to do is to slaughter their own flesh and blood for the selfish values of preserving ones family honour. The irony this sad but true story has is truly beyond belief. 'And to add salt to the wound' their daughters post mortem revealed she was still a virgin!

When one decline's reason and ignores fact, that individual becomes a possible threat to society, including the progress and advancement of intelligence, rational understanding and acknowledgment.

Questions & answers –

Abraham and his sacrifice explained

The explanation of when Abraham was told to sacrifice his only son for God was not to be sacrificed literally. The sacrifice was for Abraham to teach his son the path he must lead in Gods name. This would mean that after Abraham had done this, he must leave his son and go forth to do Gods work, resulting in them going their separate ways into distant lands to preach the word, therefore leaving the son he loved dearly and had great plans for in the values of the Earth.

Take heed that the good book was written by man who has tendencies to interoperate scenarios to their own strengths and weaknesses, as I may have!

Should we bring back the death sentence?

If society has created a monster, why should it be allowed to kill it? For example: – If a psychotic drug addict has a child and teaches it to become as itself, is killing it the cure or simply removing it from its environment and rehabilitation. Killing things is not the answer. 'Death' is not the answer. Do we not wallow in enough of this as it is? Blessed are the merciful for they shall receive mercy.

Would you give your life for another?

To give a righteous life for a non righteous person is a negative action? As a non righteous person is already recognised as being dead. If you're 'not' righteous then your action, inadvertent of death, could give favour to your next existence, as this is recognised as acting on free will.

To risk possible harm to ones self in preventing negativity with no aim of reward, therefore a reward is due. If you are righteous, then wisdom will prevail and the spiritual guidance will direct your decision to act!

HELL

Through my channelling, I have come to learn that there is a hell, just as much as there is a heaven. These are humanities words for these elements, how it works is as follows.

The whole universe works on the basis of negative and positive, good and evil. Mankind was created because the only way these elements can be enhanced is by the understanding of what you choose to do with free will. Once you have reached an enlightened stage by being righteous and using your life only for the benefit of others, you can precede to a greater spiritual existence, depending on how great your endeavours were in this existence.

This will allow you to, for example, move to the realm of Angels/benevolent energy. From that level you will enhance your enlightenment to the full aim of reaching heaven, which is the positive force/energy counter balancing the negative.

If you choose to be evil or selfish and wallow in the material temptations, neglecting those less fortunate than yourself, you will be re-incarnated into a life which is less fortunate than you're previous. This life/existence will encounter much bereavement; bereavement is given to you for enlightenment, as every negative divines you and will help you to develop yourself either way. You can use this for good/positive or to give more power to the dark forces. If you decide to go to the dark side, you will inevitably be accepted into hell, to which you will then remain for eternity to counter balance the good.

These levels are also applicable for you to reach hell, as neither of the elements can use you as a power source until you are fully charged. Basically only you can decide/chose to go to either element. If either side forces you, the power source is negative and will not enhance neither of them. Each element has its cards which can be played to sway you, only you can open your eyes to these signs. To be able to see these you must ignore material brainwashing by society, and open your mind to the truth that there are other forces at work than those that you can just feel or see.

Do not let anyone convince you otherwise, as they have fallen into the negative elements trap and will slowly be reeled into its snare.

Hell has everything you "desire", everything you can "wish for", yet has no purity, therefore all that abide there are of pure unadulterated evil.

Each day will be a battle of survival, yet you cannot die. You will fear sleep and physically and emotionally feel the pain of each attack, and these will be of the deepest unimaginable depravities. This is what keeps the furnace of hell aflame, the fire signifies pain. There cannot be a moment that suffering is not felt.

Questions & answers –

My parents used to tell me to forgive but I find it hard sometimes

It is not supposed to be easy, but this should help. When we get angry towards certain people and say, 'may you rot in hell', in the spiritual realm and in regards to the balance of our world it is truly the last thing we want to happen. Our quest while we are here is to convert all evil people to become good.

The reason why is fully explained in this book. The world works through negative and positive energies, therefore the more bad people who go to the negative side, 'commonly known as hell'; help to make it a stronger force against us, therefore the above condemnation of them condemns oneself. This is also explained scientifically via the theory of the atom as explained.

IS THERE A BEGINNING AND END OF THE WORLD

To put it into perspective, it is like asking where the world's edge is. We know there isn't, we continue to go round, 'unless we change direction'! If we can propel ourselves upwards, 'then' the edge lies wherever you stand, you are on the edge at all times, meaning, 'you' create the edge.

The beginning and the end lies within us, as we are the creators of our surroundings, the creators of our own world and existence.

A scientific explanation starts with a 'false vacuum', which simplified means we are created from nothing! Even though the fundamental laws of physics state that energy cannot be created from nothing, this law hasn't actually been broken. While it is true that all the matter you have 'created' does have positive energy, we know from Einstein's relativity that gravity has negative energy. Therefore if you were to add up all the positive energy/matter and then minus the negative energy/gravity, you would have a result of zero. Therefore creating nothing at all. (*Professor Guth*)

Everything we see is created by the energies of everything, be it our emotions, clashing of rocks and of the smallest of things (atoms). In regards to emotions, this means those you can see and those you can't. For example, if someone punches you, you feel the pain, likewise, if you lose someone you love, you also feel the pain.

As a material view, this would suggest that 'Earth' was created from either external negative emotions, or the natural crashing of energies which would still be regarded as negative due to its destructive nature. I have mentioned negative due to the destructive elements of our earth, be it the devouring of a life for another and the constant weather and plate movements.

LIFE AFTER DEATH

When you die your energy on earth caries on like the light from a dead star. The star we see may have died millions of years ago, yet we will continue seeing it and its light will continue to affect its surroundings. When the light of the star dies, it then continues in a different form, not knowing of its previous existence, as that is no longer. As an explanation, whilst the light was emitting from the star it was also creating and giving life, example: - the seed of a tree becomes a tree, basically the seed changes form and takes on a new existence.

You are currently a solid star, when you die your energy 'not your soul' will remain and continue to affect the earths balance. You plant your life's seed on earth based on the way you live, which will then give birth to good or bad fruit.

Another example: - Picture a wheel lying on the floor motionless, you are standing above looking down at it, both are connected 'the wheel and you'. Your life at present is the person standing looking at the wheel, you then pick up the wheel, balance it and push it to get it started on a role. This action represents your life after death, meaning, the life force of the being pushing the wheel dies and passes onto the motion of the wheel, these are the differences of both existences.

Many wise men try to identify the afterlife as many different levels which are achieved by the actions you take in this present lifetime. They try to convince you that you move on from this world into a spiritual one outside of earth's realm. A more exact interpretation, it is true that the life you are leading at present, if not pure, will carve out a next life/existence for you, answering the question to who is God? As a simplified answer, 'You are'. Therefore you cannot hide anything from yourself, be it an action or an emotion. If you do not know how to differentiate a just action from a negative one then you must try to seek out a recognised righteous man to advise you, otherwise await my next book as a complete guide.

As stated, a 'level' will incorporate all the positive and negative elements attributed to you in this lifetime. As when you pass on, you are reincarnated into your own creation of a self structured world. This **'is'** one of those lives/levels, everything your five senses acknowledge is of YOUR creation.

You must also be aware that if you cannot differentiate between just and wrong, the creative elements of our whole being would still dictate the outcome, as these are the elements in which our existence is made of, positive and negative. It is impossible to avoid or escape these elements as it is to escape yourself.

A recent experiment in 2008 on the subject of sleep revealed that if the bedroom smells bad it contributes to bad dreams, if it smells good it results in good dreams. This proves that the subconscious absorbs elements outside of your acknowledgment, creating energies which will eventually accumulate into the outcome of an afterlife.

Next time you cuss God; think again as you cuss yourself, and if your life is a mess then blame no other. Paradise is yours; all it takes is the simple task of being good, this means to conform to the natural elements of your existence. If you do not want to do what's right, then suffer your own justification.

Recognise all mankind and non terrestrial life as being your children. Your actions towards them should be the same as you would take as a loving parent.

The death of mankind and non terrestrial life is a negative element to your next existence.

The death of any other form of life will be a negative element to the material world, earth, including your next earth.

Not just actions but also emotions of both elements will also act towards our world and your next.

All stated fit into one category, treat everyone and everything as you and your loved ones wish to be treated.

A brief and simple example, next time an individual upsets you to a point of retaliation, imagine that person being your own family member, and visualise the assault as if on a son, daughter, mother ect. Master your own emotions and walk away or the fault will be yours to add to the negative load one currently carries.

This will also explain those who experience re-incarnation. What happens is when you die in this lifetime, all the emotional content of your life and negative/positive elements create your next existence. That world can be based on this one, as this is what your subconscious/data bank stores. Much of it can be the same, when just as much will not; this is why re-incarnated individuals will always find a fault in what they recall.

Another example of life after death is this, imagine wearing a dream machine, this is a mask that you wear when going to sleep that is supposed to work like this: - when we dream our eyes flutter at a faster rate, this then notifies the mask which switches on a red light onto your eyelid. Within your dream state you notice the red light which notifies your mind that you are in a dream. At this stage you can take full control of your dream. This applies to real life; I am your light notifying you that you can be in full control of it by believing in all those elements which society has convinced you not to. It will then, on a spiritual level, be possible for you to achieve a Neo ability in a Matrix existence.

THE ONLY WAY DIRECTLY INTO HEAVEN

Avoid possessions, become love, this can in many cases be envisaged by the love of a pet dog, as no matter how harshly it is treated it swiftly forgives and showers you with love.

As much as you may love your family and friends, do not allow them to distract you from you true purpose, as your participation in life is to serve others and preach the word of peace.

Heaven/your future existence, will then give in return an eternal life of happiness; you will be in a place in time where in life you were at your happiest with an overwhelming sense of safety and peace beyond any known feeling you can experience. Do not try to rationalise it, as you cannot rationalise what you cannot comprehend. The afterlife has no time and space, neither are you inhibited to one dimension or a single place. In this state, "Heaven", you do not own anything but you have everything.

Many believe if they do well here by helping the less fortunate, it is enough, as they have put their notability and money to good causes. I am sorry to say it is not that simple. Imagine a forest full of trees as far as the eye can see; now imagine you have a fireplace which can only be stoked with firewood. Picture the trees being those you have helped, the trees are good for they will purify our world and give life to many creatures, continuing the survival of this planet. This is a good thing as when a righteous person passes on he leaves a positive energy which helps to stabilise Earth. But none of these trees can be used to stoke the fire, the fire being Heaven.

Heaven is in search of positive energy to keep the fire burning. The only thing that can do this is firewood; firewood is one who has no thought for themselves and is only here to serve those in need and convert the bad doers into good/peace.

If you do not do the above you will be recycled to try again. This means that when you die you lose everything on earth, including everyone you know. You will not see/recognise passed friends and family ever again until you reach that goal. All that will happen is you will start again with different events that are being carved by you by what you do today. To prevent this, all one needs to do is to believe in the Divine and every action should be sincere and just. Not because it is according to civil and moral laws but because it is according to the Divine laws and the natural elements of our existence. But most importantly, convert the faithless into faith, destruction into peace. By this action you will be part of Heaven.

I reiterate, the fire cannot be fuelled by the trees, 'charitable'. If there are only the charitable, the fire dies; only firewood, the servant, can do this! Take heed, to be meek as in charitable, in the principle of using your effort and money to help mankind, will help Earth, not the heavenly force/positive energy.

Another example, if a person is about to commit suicide and 'you' prevent it, it is recognised that you have saved a life, 'saved a tree as stated above'. Yet a life cannot be truly saved unless the person saved chooses to convert his life into doing good by the means of never harming anything emotionally nor physically, and converting others to do the same. The person is only then saved and becomes 'firewood'.

Do not let this dishearten or hinder your efforts to do good deeds, the positive elements in your life towards others will enhance your next existence and your future happiness is created by good deeds.

My knowledge of our next life has been enhanced due to a personal outer body experience. I found myself slowly moving away from my body, my first emotion was panic, thoughts of family and friends, grasping to come back, as I continued I began to distance myself slightly from earth and become confused and split between where I wanted to go, as I was drawn to a new home, my true place of being. I then had great feelings of relief, as an understanding of where I was and why, this I have now relayed to you.

When prophets and people tell you they have been to Heaven and proceed to tell you what it is like, they describe their own personal Heaven. There is no fixed Heaven as there is for example your home, as Heaven is created within every individual. The only thing you should take heed of is how it works in regards to how it is affected by your present actions and beliefs in life.

THE END – FOR NOW!

I am not a preacher, as you will only listen to what you want to hear. I am a shepherd of your belief, a sower of seeds. Ask not who I am, as do you not recognise yourself when you look upon your reflection. There are many of you in this world, yet there are so few if any. Why do I bother doing this you ask? When a storm washed thousands of starfish upon a shore and two people walked amongst them, and one every so often picked one up to throw it back into the sea, the other said, 'why are you doing this as it is not going to make any difference to so many', the other replied, 'it made a difference to that one'. Live your life, for this is your purpose but remember, time is like a grain of sand on an everlasting beach, but to live it in peace and harmony one will become the beach and be eternal. Understand when you harm another being you harm yourself. You live for your afterlife not for this one.

Do not harm your enemies or those who inflict terrible atrocities upon you, as they do this to themselves. Have pity on them as they do not know what they do.

Do not fall into the devils web as his spawn is within us, it's our revenge, anger, jealousy, pride and greed which will allow it to hatch and devour our souls.

We, I, you, have the power to change all the negative elements of this world into positive; do not blame any one else for the good you do not do yourself.

The simplicity of all your quests and answers lay dormant within you. You are your own destiny and the destiny of our world – **YOU!!**

John the Baptist
'Listen to one man crying in the wilderness'.

Question your own interpretation of what is good, if it entails doing a negative action to achieve that goal, does this not make you also part of the evil.

The battle against evil begins and ends with **YOU!!**

Please do not condemn or worship me for what is written, as I am only the messenger.

If you believe this book can help mankind and wish to be part of the positive elements it may have, inform others to read it.

Thank you for helping make the world a better place.

May the blessings in life be yours, now and forever.

To quote Matthew regarding my sentiments: - *Do not think that I have come to abolish the Law or the Prophets; I have not come to abolish them but to fulfill them.*

Matthew 5:17

These writings will be left behind for all generations as something to ridicule for the many, but enlightenment and eternal life of joy for the few.

There will be another book to follow giving a complete guide in differentiating and understanding positive actions from negative, and how to separate these actions from what mainstream society has taught you.

If you wish to be informed of its publication please leave your contact details via this email.

thewiselisten@yahoo.co.uk

Proceeds from the sale of this book will go towards distribution, charities and the continuous teaching and understanding of peace.

Beatitudes

Blessed are the poor in spirit,
for theirs is the kingdom of heaven.

Blessed are they who mourn,
for they shall be comforted.

Blessed are the meek,
for they shall inherit the earth.

Blessed are they who hunger and thirst for righteousness,
for they shall be filled.

Blessed are the merciful,
for they shall obtain mercy.

Blessed are the pure of heart,
for they shall see God.

Blessed are the peacemakers,
for they shall be called children of God.

Blessed are they which are persecuted for righteousness sake, for theirs is the kingdom of heaven. Blessed are ye when men shall revile you and persecute you and shall say all manner of evil against you falsely for my sake, rejoice and be exceeding glad, for great is your reward in heaven for so persecuted they the prophets which were before you.

What are we?

We are simply a process of combined thought.

If you are currently in the dark to the natural elements of existence, reading this book will enlighten your subconscious, meaning, it will be as if switching on a light in a presently dark room.

If you fear awakening a dormant part of the mind, then do not read this book.

Published by – Pino Deufemia

Author – Pino Deufemia

And they that be wise shall shine as the brightness of the firmament; and they that turn many to righteousness as the stars for ever and ever.

Daniel 12:3

www.ingramcontent.com/pod-product-compliance
Lightning Source LLC
Chambersburg PA
CBHW032021040426
42448CB00006B/695